W9-AQE-363

ONE YEAR LATER

ONE YEAR LATER

An Assessment of the Nation's Response to the Crisis Described by the National Advisory Commission on Civil Disorders

URBAN AMERICA, INC.
AND THE URBAN COALITION

FOREWORDS BY

John W. Gardner

AND

Terry Sanford

FREDERICK A. PRAEGER, *Publishers*
New York • Washington • London

FREDERICK A. PRAEGER, *Publishers*
111 Fourth Avenue, New York, N.Y. 10003, U.S.A.
5, Cromwell Place, London S.W.7, England

Published in the United States of America in 1969
by Frederick A. Praeger, Inc., Publishers

Library of Congress Catalog Card Number: 71-82148

Printed in the United States of America

Foreword by John W. Gardner

Chairman, The Urban Coalition

One year ago, the National Advisory Commission on Civil Disorders described in compelling terms the gravity of the human problems facing the United States. The Commission's Report brought into sharp focus the social and economic inequities that, for too long, have blighted the lives of many Americans.

One year later, this report, prepared by Urban America and the Urban Coalition, makes it clear that the nation's response to the crisis of the cities has been perilously inadequate.

America has made a start—but only a start—on what the Commission described as the "major unfinished business of this Nation." But it has not made the total commitment that is so urgently needed if it is to make a livable society for every American.

The building of a better America will require a far greater commitment of its resources and energies. More importantly, it will require a far greater commitment of national will.

Foreword by Terry Sanford

President, Urban America, Inc.

This report attempts to measure a year in the nation's history against the findings of the National Advisory Commission on Civil Disorders. The most sobering of the report's conclusions, however, concern the future rather than the immediate past.

It is too much to expect that problems of the depth and gravity of those described by the Commission could be solved in a single year. What this report looks for are the beginnings of progress toward the Commission's overall goal—a just and unified society. What it finds is that the nation has yet to adopt this goal and shape the strategies necessary to achieve it. It seems content to let the future happen, largely without agreement on its design or direction.

The danger of this drift was spelled out by the Commission and is underscored by the year-after findings. America faces a period of unprecedented growth and with it, inevitably, major change. If growth follows the pattern of the past, change will be entirely in the direction of further social division. A population study cited in this report projects a picture of America in 1985: It is an America of swollen metropolitan areas, black at the core and white at the fringes, with its problems—particularly those of the education and employment of minority youth—expanded beyond hope of solution.

No choice is required to make this picture reality. All the nation has to do is fail to make a choice, and the pieces will fall inexorably into place.

There are alternatives. There is nothing in law or tradition to say that a nation cannot take a hand in its future. The force of growth can be used to heal a society, to unify it. The impending population increase, we are told, will require the nation virtually to duplicate its entire stock of physical facilities—all of the houses, buildings, roads, utilities, and other elements of the man-made environment. Americans can build this second America in such a way as to bring hope and choice and unity.

But first they must want to. The nation must begin by facing the harsh facts about the present—in particular, the poverty and injustice that are daily facts of slum-ghetto life—and the harsher prospects for the crowded future. It must determine that, this time, no group shall be left behind the progress that growth can bring and that there will be no subsociety limited in its choices to the oldest neighborhoods and least rewarding jobs.

Then, the nation must make specific plans to achieve these objectives. Two sets of strategies will be required: one to improve the lives of those now caught in the slums and ghettos; the second to see that, in the process of building the second America, no new slums and ghettos are created. Initial specifications for both sets of strategies are contained in the Civil Disorders Commission recommendations and are summarized in this report.

Acknowledgments

The National Advisory Commission on Civil Disorders made its report to the President and the nation on March 1, 1968. This is an assessment of where we stand a year later in relation to the Commission's diagnosis and warnings: whether the nation is closer to, or further from, the specter of social division raised by the Commission; whether the broad changes of attitudes, priorities, and policies advocated by the Commission have been made. It is not a measurement of the over-all national problems of poverty, of race relations, of the cities; rather, it concentrates, as did the Commission, on the convergence of all these problems on the slums and ghettos, where the civil disorders have occurred. It is, in a sense, an annual report of the nation's domestic crisis, as defined by the Commission; an attempt to determine where we are and where we seem to be heading in terms of our troubled urban centers.

The contents were prepared by the staffs of The Urban Coalition and Urban America Inc., independent nonprofit organizations which collaborate in stimulating action on urban problems. They were reviewed by a panel consisting of Jack T. Conway, president of the Center for

Community Change; Washington, D.C., attorney David Ginsburg; U.S. Senator Fred Harris (D., Okla.); New York Mayor John V. Lindsay; Dan Parker, president of the Parker Pen Co.; the Rev. Channing Phillips, Democratic national committeeman for the District of Columbia; and Tom Wicker, chief of the Washington bureau of *The New York Times.* The panel served as a valuable resource of information and judgment; it was not asked to take responsibility for the report's conclusions.

Administrative director for the report project was Brian Duff, vice president for communications of The Urban Coalition. Author of the report was Donald Canty, director of Urban America's Information Center and editor of its magazine CITY. The research and editorial staff consisted of Lois Craig, Lisa Hirsh, Gail Miller, Phyllis Myers, and Jamie Rosenthal.

Contents

ONE YEAR LATER

PART I

The Slums and Ghettos

"The civil peace has been shattered in a number of cities," said President Lyndon B. Johnson on July 29, 1967, at the first meeting of the National Advisory Commission on Civil Disorders. He then presented the Commission with its charge, in three terse questions: "What happened? Why did it happen? What can be done to prevent it from happening again and again?"

The Commission's response, delivered in its report of March 1, 1968, centered strongly on where it had happened. It found that the civil disorders "involved Negroes acting against local symbols of white American society, authority, and property in Negro neighborhoods—rather than against persons." The neighborhoods in which violence was concentrated were characterized, in nearly all instances, by poverty and social distress: They were thus slums, places of degradation; and also ghettos, places of racial confinement.

Here also were concentrated the three forces that the Commission identified as the basic causes of civil disorder:

First, "the continuing exclusion of great numbers of Negroes from the benefits of economic progress through discrimination in employment and education and their enforced confinement in segregated housing and schools. The corrosive and degrading effects of this condition and the attitudes that underlie it are the source of deepest bitterness and lie at the center of the problem of racial disorder."

Second, "the massive and growing concentration of impoverished Negroes in our major cities resulting from Negro migration from the rural South, rapid population growth, and the continuing movement of the white middle class to the suburbs. The consequence is a greatly increased burden on the already depleted resources of cities, creating a growing crisis of deteriorating facilities and services and unmet human needs."

Third, in the urban ghettos, "segregation and poverty have intersected to destroy opportunity and hope and to enforce failure. The ghettos too often mean men and women without jobs, families without men, and schools where children are processed instead of educated, until they return to the street—to crime, to narcotics, to dependency on welfare, and to bitterness and resentment against society in general and white society in particular."

It was the convergence of these three forces which the Commission said had brought about the "explosive mixture" that had built up in the slums and ghettos in postwar years. The Commission cited several reasons why the explosions had occurred when they did: frustration of hopes raised by judicial and legislative victories; a climate that legitimized violence; preachment of violence by some militant blacks; a growing sense of powerlessness among slum-ghetto residents; provocative behavior by police. These helped provide the sparks, but the explosive itself, the Commission made clear, was the destructive impact of the slums and ghettos on the people forced to live in them.

Outside, in the larger society, "most whites and many Negroes have prospered to a degree unparalleled in the history of civilization," have been able to develop "the inner resources which give life meaning," the Commission said. Inside the slums and ghettos, "it is rare that either aspiration is achieved." Television has given the slums and ghettos windows to the world outside, the Commission pointed out, making it all the harder to take the disparity.

The Commission's report gave the nation a window looking inward, invited the nation to examine the daily conditions of urban life for millions whom society had succeeded in rendering largely invisible. On the following pages is another look, a year later, at these conditions in three categories of need: poverty, education, and environment.

1. *Poverty*

Poverty, intensified in extent and impact by racial discrimination, is the most pervasive fact of life in the slums and ghettos. The Commission used Social Security Administration data from 1964 to show that 30.7 per cent of nonwhite families in central cities, as opposed to 8.8 per cent of white families, lived in poverty—on less than $3,335 per year for a family of four. Poverty was twice as prevalent among nonwhite families with female than with male heads, and a quarter of all nonwhite families were without a father in the home. Just over half the nonwhite poor in the cities were children under 16.

A prime cause of poverty in the slums and ghettos is the difficulty of finding a decent job. The unemployment rate for Negroes in 1967, the Commission reported, was 8.2 per cent. But it cited a 1966 Labor Department survey which showed that, while the unemployment rate was 7.3 per cent for all Negroes and 3.3 per cent for whites, in the "disadvantaged areas" of nine cities it was 9.3 per cent. The Labor Department also estimated that two and one-half times the number unemployed were "underemployed"—part-time workers looking for full-time jobs, full-time workers earning less than $3,000, or dropouts from the labor force.

The Commission also examined the quality of jobs available to Negroes. It found that Negro men are three times as likely as whites to be in unskilled or service jobs (based on 1966 Census Bureau figures). The concentration of male Negro employment at the lowest end of the occupational scale, the Commission said, is "the single most important source of poverty among Negroes."

The Commission identified employment problems as a key contributor to family instability: In 1967, it reported, the proportion of nonwhite men divorced and separated was more than twice as high among the unemployed as the employed. It found the number of nonwhite families headed by females increasing, especially among the poor; by 1966, among nonwhite families earning less than $3,000, 42 per cent had female heads. "With the father absent and the mother working," the Commission said, "many ghetto children spend the bulk of their time on the streets—the streets of a crime-ridden, violence-prone, and poverty-stricken world." When they reach their teens, many stay on the streets.

In the first nine months of 1967, the Commission reported, the unemployment rate among nonwhite teenagers was 26.7 per cent. It was an age group the Commission found well represented among the participants in civil disorders.

Welfare is the major public program aimed at poverty in the slums and ghettos. But the Commission found that the welfare system "contributes materially to the tensions and social disorganization that have led to civil disorders." The Commission cited two critical deficiencies in the system: "First, it excludes large numbers of persons who are in great need, and who, if provided a decent level of support, might be able to become more productive and self-sufficient. Second, for those who are included, it provides assistance well below the minimum necessary for a humane level of existence and imposes restrictions that encourage continued dependency on welfare and undermine self-respect." The welfare system's failures, said the Commission, "alienate the taxpayers who support it, the social workers who administer it, and the poor who depend on it."

Basic strategies

The Commission's recommended war on poverty in the slums and ghettos went beyond any one agency of government and was planned on four distinct fronts. The first and largest was employment; the second, economic development of poverty areas and encouragement of ghetto business ownership; the third, reform of the present welfare system; and the fourth (eventually, perhaps, the most costly), a national system of income supplementation.

In employment, the Commission proposed creating two million new jobs in the next three years, assigning a million each to the public and private sectors. It suggested that many of the public-sector jobs could be created quickly at the local level, "where there are vast unmet needs in education, health, recreation, public safety, sanitation, and other municipal services"; and that they could provide the first step toward private-sector jobs and futures. The additional private-sector jobs would be developed with public encouragement, through a Congressionally chartered corporation or tax credits. On-the-job training and special help for the hard-core unemployed would be built into both the public and private programs. In addition, the Commission called for greatly intensified enforcement of laws against discrimination in hiring and promotion.

Tax credits also were the recommended device for

enticing business and industry into poverty areas—both urban, where they would ease unemployment, and rural, where they would stem migration. The Commission's brief treatment of ghetto entrepreneurship emphasized a more generous and more socially relevant role for the Small Business Administration through expansion of its loan and loan-guarantee programs.

The Commission's "overhaul" of the welfare system also had four objectives. They were to "(a) provide more adequate levels of assistance on the basis of uniform national standards; (b) reduce the burden on state and local government by financing assistance costs almost entirely with federal funds; (c) create new incentives to work and eliminate the features that cause hardship and dependency; and (d) improve family-planning and other social services to welfare recipients." The Commission called for an outright repeal of the 1967 Congressional freeze on the number of Aid For Dependent Children recipients (originally to have taken effect in 1968 but postponed a year). With respect to another 1967 amendment requiring welfare recipients to take job training, the Commission suggested that Congress make its intent more achievable by providing more training opportunities and more day-care centers, and allowing recipients to keep more of their pay without losing benefits.

The Commission's "longer-range strategy" was to put a floor under the incomes of all Americans. It did not choose between alternate forms of income supplements, but proposed two basic purposes: "To provide for those who can work or who do work any necessary supplements in such a way as to develop incentives for fuller employment; [and] to provide for those who cannot work, and for mothers who decide to remain with their children, a minimum standard of decent living. . . ." The cost, the Commission acknowledged, would be substantial: "Yet if the deepening cycle of poverty and dependence on welfare can be broken, if the children of the poor can be given the opportunity to scale the wall that now separates them from the rest of society, the return on this investment will be great indeed."

One year later

The cycle of poverty in the slums and ghettos has been slowed by the counterforce of the whirring economy. Unemployment is down and income is up, even in the hardest-to-reach places and categories of people. But the cycle of dependence, measured by the number of welfare recipients, has accelerated more than the Commission anticipated.

This seeming paradox, partially due to special forces at work in the world of welfare, raises two questions: How much economic progress is enough to change the life-system of the slums and ghettos? The Commission pointed out that "poverty in an affluent society is more than absolute deprivation. . . . Relative deprivation—inequality—is a more useful concept. . . ." Has the redress of inequality, in terms of jobs and income, kept up with the rise of expectations and resentment?

The Commission had estimated that in 1964, 30.7 per cent of Negroes in central cities lived in poverty. A Census Bureau study, released in February of this year, showed the 1967 figure to be an even 30 per cent. The census used 1959 as a point of comparison, and the figure then was 43 per cent. Against this progress it pointed out that the 1967 incidence of Negro poverty in the cities was three times that of whites.

Negro family income in the cities also had risen sharply in the nine years to a median of $5,623, but was 68 per cent of white family income. A third of Negro families in the cities lived on $4,000 a year or less; 16 per cent of whites did. More than two-thirds of Negro families in the cities lived on $8,000 a year or less; less than half of whites did. Education did not reduce the disparity: Blacks with eight years or less of school had incomes 75 per cent of whites with the same; black college graduates had incomes 74 per cent of their white counterparts. Black college graduates earned only $13 more per year, at the median, than white high school graduates.[1]

In employment, more precise data is available now than at the time the Commission was assembling its report. The Department of Labor has instituted a quarterly survey of unemployment in "poverty neighborhoods" of the nation's 100 largest cities—the fifth of the census tracts that rank lowest on an index of income, education, skills, housing, and proportion of broken families derived from the 1960 census. These quarterly reports show steady and substantial progress during 1968. They also show wide and continuing gaps between the employment status of whites and Negroes.

First, as a benchmark, these were the nationwide statistics for fourth-quarter 1967 and 1968 in metropolitan areas of 250,000 or more population:[2] In 1967, the over-all unemployment rate was 3.7 per cent in these metropolitan areas. Among whites it was 3.2 per cent and among Negroes 7 per cent (already a gain from the Commission's figures). By 1968, the over-all rate had declined to 3.2 per cent; for whites, 2.8 per cent, and for Negroes, 6.1 per cent. The gain for Negroes had been largest; the 6.1 per cent figure was the lowest since 1953.

But, as the Commission pointed out, 6 per cent unemployment in the general economy means recession. Even the 1968 figures, then, showed whites in the large metropolitan areas to be in the midst of historic prosperity and blacks in recession.

Now focusing on the poverty neighborhoods (read slums and ghettos) of the 100 cities:[3] In the fourth quarter of 1967, they had an over-all unemployment rate of 6.9 per cent, compared to 3.2 per cent in other urban neighborhoods. Among whites it was 5.4 per cent in poverty neighborhoods and 3 per cent outside. Among Negroes it was 9 per cent in poverty neighborhoods and 5.8 per cent outside.

By 1968, the over-all unemployment rate in poverty neighborhoods had declined to 5.2 per cent and in other urban neighborhoods to 2.8 per cent. Among whites it was 4.4 per cent in poverty neighborhoods and 2.5 per cent outside. Among blacks it was 6.4 per cent in poverty neighborhoods and 5.2 per cent outside. Improvement in the lot of the slum-ghetto blacks had been dramatic in both absolute and relative terms; they had accounted for all but 1 per cent of the progress in poverty neighborhood employment. But again, for perspective, they had risen from a distress-level 9 per cent to recession-level 6.4. Also, a Negro in a poverty neighborhood remained twice as likely to be unemployed as the generality of workers in large metropolitan areas. No similar comparative measurement is available of underemployment or subemployment, which the Commission found to be a multiple of the unemployment problem.

A final close-in look: Black teenagers in poverty neighborhoods, in the final quarter of 1967, had an unemployment rate of a staggering 34 per cent, worse than even the Commission had estimated. By 1968 it had been reduced to 27.3 per cent. The gain was highly significant, but did not remove the problem of idle youth from the streets of the slums and ghettos.

The Commission, in its concern with the quality as well as the quantity of jobs available to Negroes, suggested that "the potential income gains from upgrading the male nonwhite labor force are much larger than those from reducing nonwhite unemployment." A comparison of its 1966 data on distribution of the nonwhite work force with 1968 figures[4] shows a degree of progress in upgrading jobs well below that made in reducing unemployment. Nonwhites are still clustered at the lower end of the scale of skills and rewards:

Percentage of Male Workers in Each Type of Occupation
(figures are in per cent below)

	White		*Nonwhite*	
Occupation	*1966*	*1968*	*1966*	*1968*
Professional, Technical, Managerial	27	28.8	9	10.2
Clerical and Sales	14	13.2	9	8.8
Craftsmen and Foremen	20	20.9	12	13.4
Operatives	20	19.3	27	28.2
Service Workers	6	6.1	16	14.5
Nonfarm Laborers	6	5.9	20	18.1
Farmers and Farm Workers	7	5.9	8	6.7

In February of this year, the U.S. Equal Employment Opportunity Commission issued a 1,500-page report that fills out the Civil Disorders Commission's portrait of job inequality and identifies racial discrimination as the major cause.[5] The EEOC report was based on 1966 information from 43,000 individual employers.

"The same restrictive pattern of minority employment is repeated throughout the data," it says. "At the white collar level, minority workers are virtually excluded from managerial and professional jobs, are rarely significant in sales positions, are underrepresented among technicians and clerical. At the blue collar level, they hold less than their share of skilled craft jobs and are over-concentrated in low-status laborer and service worker jobs. Where they do participate significantly in the white collar positions they enjoy salaries and status below those usually accompanying such jobs."

EEOC has its own definition of underemployment: "the status of men and women who perform work which does not fully utilize their education, skills, and talents." From two different analyses of the reports from employers, it concludes that the lower educational level of minority groups "accounts for only about one-third of the difference in occupational ranking between Negro men and majority-group men. The inevitable conclusion," it says, "is that the other two-thirds must be attributed to discrimination, deliberate or inadvertent."

The report says that job discrimination "is strongest against Negro men in those industries which have a high proportion of Negro employees; have Negro and white employees with high average educational levels; have a high proportion of well-paying positions; or have a high proportion of their operations in the South. . . . In other words, it would seem that greater progress for Negroes brings forth progressively stronger discrimination against them. The statistical conclusions above could well be stated this way: If a large number of Negroes succeed in getting jobs in an industry, relatively fewer of them can expect promotions. If large numbers of Negroes in an industry have high educational attainment, the bias against them will be stronger. If an industry has many well-paying jobs, a relatively higher proportion of those jobs will be restricted to majority-group employees."

Negro men, the report says, "hold only 2.1 per cent of the jobs in the five industries which have the highest occupational ranking—insurance services; holding and other investment companies; non-bank credit agencies; communications; and insurance carriers. At the other end of the scale, Negro males fill 9.6 per cent of the jobs in those five industries which have the lowest occupational ranking—food trade; water transportation; motor freight and warehousing; furniture and fixtures manufacturing; and anthracite coal mining. Thus the percentage of Negro male employees in the bottom five industries is about four and a half times the percentage in the top five industries."

The EEOC report reinforces the Civil Disorders Commission's persistent warning that it will take more than continued general prosperity to lift the residents of the slums and ghettos out of poverty. Further reinforcement came in the annual economic report to the President of the Council of Economic Advisers, issued in January of this year, which devoted a chapter—a significant fact in itself—to "Combating Poverty in a Prosperous Economy." [6]

"Virtually all the progress in reducing poverty over the past 20 years has occurred during periods of general prosperity," the economic report says. "In three periods of sustained economic expansion—1949–53, 1954–56, and 1961 to the present—the annual decline in the numbers of individuals in poverty averaged two million or more a year. In contrast, during recessions the number of poor people has increased. The brief recession of 1954 wiped out half of the gains of the preceding four-year expansion. . . ."

"If the 1961–68 reductions in the number of poor persons could be continued," the economic report goes on, "poverty would be eliminated entirely in about 10 years. If the record of 1968 could be continued, poverty would be eliminated in about five and a half years. Maintenance of these rapid reductions will become increasingly difficult because, as poverty declines, an increasing fraction of the remaining poor are members of households whose economic status is least affected by prosperity. . . .

"Much of the progress in the 1960's has been due to the lowering of the unemployment rate. . . . The hard-core unemployed, the educationally disadvantaged, and the victims of discrimination are the last to be hired during a return to high employment and the first to be fired during a slowdown. Upgrading the unskilled and uneducated to fill shortages in skilled labor takes time. Consequently, if high employment is maintained, these adjustments will continue to reduce poverty, but their effects will gradually diminish. In the absence of increased direct assistance to the poor or further reductions in unemployment, present annual declines in poverty must be expected to become smaller."

Nor will the elimination of poverty come into sight "if the incomes of the poor grow only at the same pace as the incomes of other households," the report warns. "To shorten substantially the period needed to reduce poverty, the incomes of the poor must grow faster than average income. Some redistribution to the poor must be made from the benefits of growth."

The EEOC report focused on those kept out of the general prosperity by racial discrimination, the economic report on those left behind to suffer poverty amid affluence. Just as there is "structural unemployment," caused by personal and social rather than economic factors, there is "structural poverty" that does not respond to national economic growth. Both are concentrated in the slums and ghettos, and both require specific remedies of the kind proposed by the Civil Disorders Commission. Most of these remedies, a year later, remain to be effectively applied.

The Commission divided its employment goals between the public and private sectors, and between job-training and job-creation. In the past year, there was increased private-public cooperation on job training that produced measurable progress. The progress in job creation was limited, almost entirely on the private side.

Many of the Commission's job-training specifications were met by the JOBS program, which got fully underway during 1968 in the nation's 50 largest cities under the National Alliance of Businessmen. The program combines federal subsidies for training the hard-core unemployed with alliance volunteers finding or providing the training slots. Hiring began May 1, 1968, and by January 10 of this year the alliance reported that 12,500 firms had placed 125,000 persons. Of these, it said 85,000 were still on the job for a retention rate of 68 per cent.

Just under a third of these placements were under JOBS contracts for training subsidies, which averaged $2,850 per worker. For the rest, alliance employers paid all expenses (and were not bound by government training standards). Seventy-four per cent of the placements were of Negro workers, the alliance reported. The average trainee had been unemployed about half of the previous year; his combined family income had been $2,749 for a household of 3.67 persons. The alliance's second-year goal is 200,000, assuming continued prosperity.

The older Manpower Development and Training Act was extended but not expanded by Congress in 1968. It aided 125,000 trainees in the past fiscal year compared to 11,000 in fiscal 1965.[7] Currently, half of the trainees have less than four years of high school and just over half are from poverty families. The Job Corps by mid-1968 had provided food, health care, and job training for 195,000 disadvantaged youths since 1965, and the Neighborhood Youth Corps had provided part-time and summer work for more than 1.3 million enrollees in the same period. Both were cut back by Congress, and the Nixon Administration, at this writing, had not indicated whether they would be continued.

The largest gap remains in the area of public creation of additional jobs. Legislation for this purpose came within five votes of passing the Senate in 1967, after the summer disorders, but in 1968 none of several versions paralleling the Commission recommendations reached the floor of either house. All were opposed by the Johnson Administration. Some legislative observers feel there has been a steady buildup of Congressional support for the idea of "government as employer of last resort," however, and feel its enactment into law may not be too remote a prospect.

Job discrimination was the target of increased voluntary efforts in 1968. The National Association of Manufacturers at year's end began a continuing series of four-day conferences around the country with the cooperation of the Equal Employment Opportunity Commission.

EEOC, limited in powers, had also made some progress in enforcement of anti-discrimination laws, but it was progress that started very near the point of zero.

The Civil Rights Act of 1964 allows the government to cancel contracts with firms who practice discrimination. No contract has ever been cancelled, and it was not until May, 1968, that the first proceeding was started to ban a firm from future federal contracts under provisions of the act.[8] Every year since 1964 legislation has been introduced in Congress to permit the Equal Employment Opportunity Commission to issue cease-and-desist orders and require reinstatement or hiring of aggrieved would-be workers in discrimination cases. Every year it has been defeated, and was again in 1968. The NAACP won a significant suit under the act in October, in which a federal court found the electrical workers union in Cincinnati had practiced discrimination and ordered it to change its hiring system. Twenty-five suits were filed by the Justice Department in 1968 under the equal employment section of the 1964 act. Only 10 had been filed in all the previous years.

Dwarfed by the treatment of employment, development of Negro businesses and businessmen receives only three paragraphs in the Commission report. In the past year, the subject has received major attention from vocal black spokesmen, from the business community, from the press, and from the new President, who called it "black capitalism" in his campaign. This attention, however, has yet to be matched by widespread accomplishment, and by early 1969 there were indications that some blacks were having second thoughts about the promise of entrepreneurship.

Blacks own and operate less than 1 per cent of the

nearly five million private businesses in the country.[9] Typically, these are small, marginal businesses: retail and service firms which cater to a constricted market. There are some 20 black-owned banks (out of a national total of more than 14,000), plus 36 black savings and loan associations and 43 mortgage banks; there are about 50 black-owned life insurance companies (with combined assets of 0.2 per cent of the industry's total—and only two of which function nationally). In addition there is a small, though growing, number of black manufacturing firms. Still, fewer than 3 per cent of the 1.5 million Americans who classify themselves as self-employed are black.

Black income has grown from $3.5 billion a year in 1940 to $32 billion today, but 98 per cent of it is spent outside the black community.[10] Only seven authorized automobile dealers in the country are black.[11] And out of 500,000 construction contractors, fewer than 8,000 are black; they handle less than one half of one per cent of the $100 billion U.S. construction volume.[12]

A few of the figures are more heartening: Those seven car dealers are seven times as many as there were two years ago; new black-owned banks are in formation in seven cities. One recent study showed that in certain areas of Harlem, black business ownership has risen to 58 per cent. In Washington, too, where blacks comprise two-thirds of the population and have owned less than 7 per cent of the business,[13] there has been a change in the pattern of inner-city ownership, with blacks taking over some of the stores hit by the April riots. But it would take 400 of such transfers to up the percentage more than one point.

There are three chief factors which serve as impediments to black entrepreneurship: difficulty in obtaining capital, lack of technical expertise or know-how, and uncertain markets. Up until very recently, banks have been most reluctant to make loans to blacks, particularly those involved in high-risk ghetto ventures; and blacks are usually unable to obtain enough equity or collateral to persuade them to change their minds. Insurance, too, is a severe problem: Most ghetto businessmen can buy it only at prohibitive prices, if at all; and in a vicious circle, lack of coverage tends to mean lack of credit.

Uncertain markets are a problem which stem from the need, generally agreed upon by both blacks and whites, for black enterprise to move beyond the traditional small retail and service pattern with its limited neighborhood market and into light manufacturing and other ventures aimed at the general economy. A recent Small Business Administration report, for example, recommends a push for Negroes in frozen food processing, men's and boys' apparel, and commercial printing, among others. The change requires contacts and know-how that many potential black businessmen just don't possess.

Existing programs concentrate on the first two impediment-requirements, capital and managerial expertise, with a secondary emphasis on the problem of markets. There is no shortage of programs, either in government or the private sector; the main inadequacy seems to be lack of coordination among them, plus, of course, the inevitable limitations of funds.

The most comprehensive of these programs is lodged at SBA, which under a new administrator, Howard J. Samuels, last August launched "Project OWN," designed to help create minority-owned businesses through loans made at the rate of 10,000 a year by the end of this fiscal year, and double that rate by the end of fiscal 1970. Last fiscal year minority loans totalled only 1,700. One of the major innovations represented by the project is a proposed eventual shift from direct SBA loans to loans made through private banks with a 90-per-cent SBA guarantee. The purpose is not only to free more funds, but to bring about greater over-all involvement of the private sector, in recognition of the fact that the job of spurring development is too big for government to handle alone.

In addition to pushing for private involvement, SBA has relaxed its own loan criteria in line with the concept of "compensatory capitalism," based on the premise that higher risks can be accepted when high-priority social objectives are at stake. Calmly anticipating a rise in the default rate from 3 per cent to as high as 7 per cent, it has stressed "character, not collateral" and has encouraged private banks to follow suit. It has increased the ceiling on its Economic Opportunity Loans (the principal source of minority funding) to $350,000, while decreasing the equity investment standard from 50 per cent to 15 per cent and easing repayment schedules. It has also simplified its procedures, extending its blanket guarantee plan to the Economic Opportunity Loans in order to eliminate paperwork for the banks and thus enable them to make loans in a matter of days.

As of December, with the cooperation of the American Bankers Association (and permission of interest rates at up to 8 per cent), a reduction of almost 50 per cent in direct lending had been accomplished.[14] More importantly, in the three-month period ending at that date, minority loans totaled 1,223 for $25.6 million, an increase of 846 (224 per cent) and $19 million (288 per cent) over the same period in 1967. The private sector share in minority loans during the period had increased

605 per cent from the corresponding period in 1967, from $2 million to $14.1 million. Indicated annual rate of loans for the 1969 fiscal year was 5,000.

The Economic Development Administration's programs have been more limited, as a result of legislation which restricts its operations in many of the central cities. But through its Urban Projects Division it has increased both the total amount of its grants and the variety of its approaches over the past year. Concentrating on technical and managerial assistance, it has done so in some unusual ways—it funded, for example, the administrative costs of the Job Loan Corporation, a consortium of eight major Philadelphia banks who have made available a $2 million line of credit for minority borrowers, in return for the group's making the loans at the prime rate. The Labor Department in 1968 instituted an Experimental and Development program, which already has allotted $700,000 for managerial training and other support for the expansion and establishment of minority enterprise; $1 to $2 million more is anticipated. Special Impact projects are providing funds to black-owned businesses in Cleveland and Gary, Ind., as well as to the Bedford-Stuyvesant area, where approximately 20 firms have been developed since 1966 from grants totaling $2,900,000.

Title XI of the Housing Act of 1968 authorizes a new program of federal reinsurance against loss from riots and civil disorders for private insurance companies to encourage them to write more reasonable property insurance in the slum-ghettos—a possible solution to the insurance difficulties encountered by almost all small black businesses. New model cities regulations call for maximum utilization of local firms in projects connected with the program. In addition, the Federal Housing Administration recently eliminated the surety bond requirement on projects under $200,000, an action directly aimed at increased participation by minority builders.

Business development also is providing another avenue for private involvement in slum-ghetto problems. The Interracial Council for Business Opportunity since 1963 has provided volunteer counseling by businessmen to more than 2,000 black enterprises, and recently established a $3 million fund to guarantee bank loans to black entrepreneurs. The Menswear Retailers of America have set up an Ownership Opportunities Program, involving management counseling and a $20 million extended credit pool. Individual corporations such as Fairchild-Hiller, Aerojet-General, and Xerox have encouraged ghetto enterprise through partnership or guaranteed purchase arrangements.

A particularly hopeful surge of ghetto entrepreneurship has been among youth organizations in cities across the country, many of which started as gangs and are now involved in a variety of businesses from film-making to soul food shops. They have names like the Conservative Vice Lords (Chicago), the Mission Rebels (San Francisco), and Thugs United (New Orleans), and they also have a national organization, Youth Organizations United, which tries to round up money and technical advice. It has been an uphill effort and the stakes are high: Failure for the black youths, as for all blacks whose strivings have gone beyond jobs to business ownership, could bring a special kind of disillusionment with the American system.

Already the recognition is growing that there are limitations to the degree that black capitalism can help the black poor. SBA's Samuels made no bones about the fact that the object of Project OWN was "not to put the poor in business but to put the minorities in business." Only a very narrow segment of the black poor are involved in entrepreneurial programs at present, and even the blacks of lower-middle to middle class who are benefiting most are not large in number. Andrew Bennett, chief of the Urban Projects Division at the Economic Development Administration, put it this way: "We seize on a few glowing examples and imply somehow that it has made a difference. But we're talking about 25 million people. There's just not enough being invested to bring about change."

As discussion of Negro entrepreneurship went on, the welfare system continued to be the major growth industry of the slums and ghettos, to the despair of both officials and recipients. The growth was centered on the Aid For Dependent Children program (AFDC), the system's largest component, approaching twice the combined size of programs for the aged, blind, and otherwise handicapped or disabled.

In October, 1967, when the Commission was gathering its data, there were 5,148,000 AFDC recipients; 3,871,000 were children and roughly one million were mothers. By October, 1968, there were 5,882,000 AFDC recipients including 4,408,000 children.[15] The Commission had estimated a 686,000 annual rate of increase; its estimate proved conservative.

Similarly, the Commission reported that New York City, with the most extreme local welfare crisis, had 525,000 AFDC recipients and was adding 7,000 to 10,000 per month. New York's total welfare load hit the one million mark in January of this year and the approximate rate of increase in the AFDC rolls was 15,000 per month.[16] The one million figure was triple the number of welfare recipients in 1960.

In fiscal 1967, the total welfare cost was $6,981,511,000. In fiscal 1968, it was $8,866,220,000. It was split as follows among three levels of government: federal, $4.7 billion; state, $3 billion; local, $1.1 billion.[17]

These are large figures, but not large enough to lift the recipients of welfare above poverty. The economic report to the President for 1969 said that the level of assistance in federally aided welfare programs is nowhere above the poverty line. Monthly AFDC benefits for a family of four range among the states from a low of $40 to a high of $290. The average in mid-1968 was just over $2,000 per family; in five states it was less than $1,000.

The rise in welfare costs was not so much in the level of benefits—AFDC payments increased an average of $17 per family between mid-1967 and mid-1968—as in caseloads. It was highly selective. Between 1959 and 1968, according to the Citizens Budget Commission of New York, the increase in welfare caseloads nationally was 74.9 per cent. But caseloads in the 10 states with highest welfare benefits increased 148.7 per cent, while caseloads in the nine states and Puerto Rico with lowest benefits increased only 11.1 per cent. Similarly, the 10 high-pay states increased their share of the welfare dollar from 21.2 per cent to 30.1 per cent in the same period. The other 10 decreased their share from 30.3 per cent to 19.2 per cent.[18]

The impact of this conscience gap between states and localities is enormous. The Citizens Budget Commission contends that high welfare payments constitute a magnet to immigration in cities like New York, although others feel that the hope of employment (whether real or not) and the location of friends or relatives have more to do with where the urban immigrant settles.

The Regional Plan Association of New York, in a 1968 report, pointed out that costs of welfare and other poverty-related services had strained the budgets of cities in its area to the breaking point.[19] The major impact, however, was injustice: Sustenance, even survival, for Americans most in need remains an accident of geography.

The Regional Plan Association's point was that poverty is a national problem and should be accepted as a national responsibility. In the past year, bipartisan support for this concept grew noticeably. The outgoing Secretary of HEW, Wilbur Cohen, advocated both uniform federal standards and federal assumption of a larger financial load. Gov. Nelson Rockefeller of New York did the same in December at the Republican governors' meeting, and later repeated his support before the Administration's new Urban Affairs Council. In his first press conference, Cohen's successor, Robert H. Finch, indicated that national welfare standards were to have high Administration priority, and a Nixon advisory committee said the federal government should assume a far greater share of welfare costs.

Why are welfare loads rising in tandem with aggregate employment and income? A clue may be found in the fact that the number and proportion of Negro families in central cities headed by females continues to rise, and reached 30 per cent in 1968.[20] Of Negro families in the cities with incomes of $2,000 or less, more than half have no father in the home. Median earnings of working Negro women in central cities in 1967 were $2,197; nearly half of the Negro families headed by females in the cities lived in poverty. For these broken families the vicious cycle of inadequate income and social disorganization continues unabated by general prosperity. Welfare—AFDC—is their only recourse.

They are increasingly being reminded that it is also their right. The membership of the National Welfare Rights Organization, formed in August, 1967, doubled in its first year of operation. There are now 161 local organizations in 70 cities.[21] In New York, welfare rights groups are challenging the legality of flat grants replacing specific allowances for such things as clothing and furniture; in Philadelphia, they are challenging an intake system which they claim turns two out of three welfare applicants away; in St. Louis, they are pushing to reduce a 3,000-person waiting list for welfare aid which they say violates federal regulations requiring processing of applications in 30 days.

The focus of the welfare rights movement, and also of the Commission report, is on welfare practices as well as levels of aid. One such practice—denying AFDC assistance if there is a man living in the household, whether husband or father or not—was overturned in 1968 by the Supreme Court. The case originated in Alabama, where 20,000 children had been removed from welfare rolls by the "man in the house" rule. A Supreme Court decision is pending on state residency requirements, ruled illegal by lower-court decisions in the past year in Illinois, Delaware, Wisconsin, Pennsylvania, and the District of Columbia.

The much-resented investigative practices of welfare agencies also came under challenge in 1968. In June, a Federal District Court in Washington, D.C., ruled it unlawful to cut off welfare funds when a recipient refuses to open his home for search or investigation. And in one of his last acts as Secretary of HEW, Wilbur Cohen put forth a rule that eligibility for welfare be based on applicants' statements of need rather than on detailed examinations. His action was based partly on the experience of New York City, which had first tried the procedure on a demonstration basis, then instituted it citywide. The rule would apply to all 50 states, but requires the approval of Congress.

The widely feared 1967 amendments to federal welfare laws have yet to make their impact. The amendment requiring recipients to take training and seek jobs, or else lose their benefits, so far has separated few mothers from their homes and children, as critics at first feared. Most of the initial 50,000 persons affected in 38 states have been men: Administrative regulations require that unemployed fathers, teenagers, uncles, and other male relatives in the household be enlisted for training first. The special job training program established to take welfare referrals, known as WIN, has a fiscal 1969 budget of $94.5 million, enough to open roughly 100,000 training slots. The welfare mothers enrolled in WIN so far have been those who want job training badly enough to provide day care for their children on their own. The difficulties will come later, with the gradual shift from male to female referrals: Only $22 million is provided in fiscal 1969 for day-care purposes.[22]

The second amendment, freezing the AFDC rolls, was suspended for a year. Barring repeal, it will go into effect July 1. No state will be able to provide federal AFDC assistance to a larger percentage of its total population of children than were on its rolls January 1, 1968—no matter how population shifts from state to state, no matter how many children go hungry.

The at-least-partial replacement of welfare with some form of direct income supplementation, the Commission's "longer-range strategy," remained in 1968 an idea whose time had not quite come. But it was an idea that continued to occupy center stage in academic and professional debate and became, for the first time, the subject of empirical experiment.

Last August, the Office of Economic Opportunity began sending checks to 200 families in Trenton, New Jersey, with no strings attached except a requirement that once a month they report their full income. This spring the experiment will be expanded to include 1,000 families in New Jersey's six largest cities. Seven plans will be tried, with two key variables: the percentage of the gap between family income and poverty-level income that is guaranteed, and the percentage reduction in the amount of support as family income rises. The families will continue to receive their checks even if they leave New Jersey.

The debate involves the relative merits of family allowances, the negative income tax, and other income-guarantee plans. It should be resolved in part by the report of the President's Commission on Income Maintenance, due this fall after an 18-month investigation. Meanwhile, the largest impediment remains public fear that any form of income supplementation will reduce incentives to work. The Gallup Poll last June presented two propositions to a cross-sectional sample of the public: that the government should guarantee an income floor; and that the government should guarantee employment. Seventy-eight per cent supported guaranteed work and only 36 per cent supported guaranteed income.

2. *Education*

Education in the slums and ghettos is a failure. The Commission backed this flat assertion with evidence that "in the critical skills—verbal and reading ability—Negro students fall farther behind whites with each year of school completed." In the metropolitan Northeast, Negro students start school with slightly lower scores than whites on standard achievement tests; by sixth grade they are 1.6 grades behind, and by 12th grade 3.3 grades behind. By 12th grade, many have left: In the metropolitan areas of the North and West, a Negro student is more than three times as likely as a white to drop out of school by the time he is 17. The Commission's typical participant in civil disorders was, among his other characteristics, a high school dropout.

Most city schools are racially segregated because of patterns of residence. The Commission cited a 75-city survey by the U.S. Civil Rights Commission showing that 75 per cent of Negro elementary school students attend schools 90 per cent or more Negro, 83 per cent of white students schools that are 90 per cent or more white; a companion sampling of 15 cities showed that 84 per cent of the increase in Negro enrollment between 1960 and 1965 occurred in schools with Negro enrollments of over 90 per cent. The Commission draws from the 1966 Office of Education report "Equality of Educational Opportunity" (the source of the achievement and dropout figures above) the conclusion that racial and class segregation is harmful. Inevitably, all concerned—administrators, teachers, parents, and students—regard Negro schools in the slums and ghettos as inferior, the Commission says, and this helps insure that they are.

Therefore, they attract the least experienced, least qualified teachers: A 1963 study which ranked Chicago schools by the socioeconomic status of their neighborhoods showed that in the 10 lowest ranking schools, only 63.2 per cent of the teachers were fully certified; in the 10 highest the figure was 90.3 per cent. Teachers assigned to schools in the slums and ghettos "often begin with negative attitudes toward the students," the Commission said. "These attitudes are aggravated by serious discipline problems, by the high crime rates in areas surrounding the schools, and by the greater difficulties of teaching students with disadvantaged backgrounds." Such backgrounds produce a disproportionate number of emotionally disturbed and "problem" children, for whom too few special aids are available. Negative attitudes are reinforced—and passed on to the students. "The teachers expect little from their students," the Commission observed; "the students fulfilled the expectation."

Sheer numbers can overwhelm the teacher in a disadvantaged school. Negro school enrollments have increased faster than total Negro central city population. The Commission described the cycle: "As white students withdraw from a public school, they are replaced by greater numbers of Negro students—reflecting the fact that the Negro population is relatively younger, has more children of school age, makes less use of private schools, and is more densely concentrated that the white population." The result, in the slums and ghettos, is acute and concentrated overcrowding of inadequate school facilities. Washington, D.C., had one predominantly white high school in 1967 operating at 92.3 per cent capacity. Its predominantly Negro high schools were operating at 108.4 per cent to 127.1 per cent capacity.

"Inner-city schools are not only overcrowded, they also tend to be the oldest and most poorly equipped," reported the Commission. Teaching materials are scarce and "poorly adapted to the life-experiences of the students." Behind most of these deficiencies, the Commission said, is the fact that "our society spends less money educating ghetto children than children of suburban families." It cited a Civil Rights Commission study of state aid in 12 metropolitan areas in 1950 and 1964. In two the same amount per pupil went to central city and suburbs, and in six the suburbs got significantly more. Priorities were inverse to need.

The Commission found an atmosphere of increasing hostility around the schools of the slums and ghettos. They "often appear to be unresponsive to the community, communication has broken down, and parents are distrustful of education. . . . Since the needs and concerns of the ghetto community are rarely reflected in educational policy formulated on a citywide basis, the schools are often seen by ghetto youth as irrelevant." The sense of isolation from the making of school policy, the Commission said, "is adding to the polarization of the community."

Basic strategies

By the time the Commission report was issued, polarization already had occurred in the educational community. It was spurred in part by the Office of Education report on educational equality (known as the Coleman Report, for its author, Dr. James Coleman) and the Civil Rights Commission's follow-up "Racial Isolation in the United States." The Coleman Report seemed to indicate, and the Civil Rights Commission flatly said, that of all that had been tried in improving disadvantaged schools only class and/or racial integration seemed to affect the bleak statistics of underachievement. Neither report found evidence that so-called "compensatory" programs helped. Since they appeared at a time when the nation was investing substantially for the first time in compensatory education, and integration was being despaired of or abandoned as a goal, the rebuttals to the reports were swift and anguished.

The National Advisory Commission's strategies took a middle ground. On the one hand, the Commission declared: "We support integration as the priority education strategy because it is essential to the future of American society. We have seen in this last summer's disorders the consequences of racial isolation. . . . It is indispensable that opportunities for interaction between the races be expanded." The Commission recommended tougher enforcement of laws prohibiting segregation, increased aid (including bonus payments) to school systems working to end segregation, and use of such innovations as educational parks, superior "magnet" schools, and specialized education centers.

On the other hand, the Commission recognized "that

the growing dominance of pupils from disadvantaged minorities in city school populations will not seem to be reversed." It declared: "If existing disadvantages are not to be perpetuated, we must improve dramatically the quality of ghetto education. Equality of results with all-white schools in terms of achievement must be the goal." It recommended a variety of improvement programs including teacher training, year-round education for the disadvantaged, smaller classes, and more emphasis on minority-group history in curricula and textbooks.

The Commission's third strategy was to build "new links . . . between the schools and the communities they serve." It recommended that schools serve as community centers and that local residents be used as teacher aides and tutors. The Commission took note that urban school systems had become "highly centralized," found this had both good and bad aspects, and suggested another middle-road approach of "maintaining centralized control over educational standards and the raising of revenue, while decentralizing control over other aspects of educational policy." The precise mix, it said, "must be determined locally."

One year later

The indictment of failure passed on education in the slums and ghettos is just as valid and even more familiar. But the ferment stirred by the two earlier education reports and accelerated by the Commission report has increased to the point where it is rocking—in some instances, even toppling—the educational establishment. Unlike other drives for change in the schools, this one looks as if it will not end with talk: There is a discernible shift to action—clarification of strategies, heightened conflict, perhaps the beginnings of genuine change.

Not all of the turmoil is progress. Frustration has taken its toll, and any remedy that offers the glimmer of reaching the disadvantaged is seized upon. As in the larger society of which the schools are part, the dilemma is whether changes that accentuate, rather than mitigate, polarization are a necessary prelude to coming together on an equal footing—indeed, whether there is any choice.

At present the dilemma centers on community control of schools, raised by blacks in the slums and ghettos to an urgency well beyond the Commission's careful treatment of "decentralization." The major battleground, of course, was in New York City, where experiments in community control have unleashed a bitter power struggle and surfaced a nightmare of ethnic and racial hatreds. Despite the tragic public conflict, there were stories, perhaps premature in their optimism, that in the schools themselves a new atmosphere, with new methods and new teachers, was "turning on" previously alienated students. In Washington, a lesser-known experiment in community control resulted in an upturn in reading scores despite a chaotic first year, and the school has settled into an innovative but orderly second.

Elsewhere, decentralization of the schools was being widely talked about and only tentatively and less widely tried. In Chicago, an experimental four-school subdistrict was set up with a board representing the central board, the University of Chicago, and local community groups to make decisions about how federal funds are used. In 13 Los Angeles schools, a local board of parents, teachers, and students has "critical" authority over budgets and the use of materials and teachers. In Boston, several schools have in effect been pulled out of the city system and are run by a local board receiving funds from the State of Massachusetts.

Many questions remain. On the plus side, both decentralization and community control answer directly the problem of alienation by offering a meaningful relinkage of parents and community with what goes on inside the schools which, if the theory is correct, will both improve the education of the ghetto kids and renew the community in the fullest sense. It offers real change, responsibility, and accountability.

The dangers, however, are just as obvious. Will drawing new lines around communities, setting up local boards, reinforce the very segregation and isolation that the Commission warned against? What is the larger public interest and how is it expressed? When do confrontations become counterproductive, creating a dangerous new problem that once again turns us away from the children?

In a study of 13 cities prepared for The Urban Coalition, the authors found a wide variety of mechanisms by which parents have been involving themselves meaningfully in school decision-making, suggesting perhaps that the gradation of alternatives between a centralized board and total community control have not been fully examined.[23] The authors say that the rhetoric of control is more widespread than its practice; few parents really want to "run" their schools. But they do want something called "accountability," where they can look at and assess what the schools are accomplishing.

Part of the rhetoric of community control is disdain for the goal of integration. Resisted by the white community, it now has few public friends among the vocal blacks. Swamped by the publicity for the separatist push, however, desegregation efforts have gone on, both at the federal level, and more importantly, in cities and towns across the nation where individuals and organizations have persisted in fighting for it. Mostly, these efforts, both federal and grass roots, are in smaller and moderate sized cities, where distance and numbers make for a more manageable game.

A number of communities adopted desegregation plans in the past year: Niagara Falls, N.Y.; Evansville, Ind.; San Mateo, Calif.; Providence, R.I. The most dramatic, comprehensive integration plan was installed in 1968 in Berkeley, Calif., a city of 125,000 with an over-all population 25 per cent black and a school population 41 per cent black. After a decade-long community struggle, led in most recent years by peripatetic school superintendent Neil V. Sullivan, the elementary program last year moved 2,000 white children and 2,000 black out of a total of 5,000. Each of the 14 elementary schools reflects roughly the over-all racial percentage. Reports out of Berkeley are optimistic: The added costs are less than 3 per cent of the budget; predictions of teachers resigning and whites fleeing are not proving out; intensive community relations and teacher training programs are underway.

In most other cities, integration plans are more limited or voluntary; within city boundaries, there is bussing and rezoning often on the basis of equalizing crowding, which incidentally also reshuffles some black and white bodies. In Providence, a ghetto school was made into a special academically oriented school and is now 70 per cent white with a long waiting list. More plans for a moving inner-city children out to the suburbs have cropped up and existing ones have been expanded. Boston's groundbreaking operation now busses 850 children to 20 communities. New Haven and Waterbury followed Hartford's example and joined Connecticut's Project Concern, which last year moved about 800 Negro and Puerto Rican children into two dozen suburban communities. Hartford's parochial schools set up a parallel program. In Rochester, N.Y., 10 per cent of inner-city nonwhite kids were moved outward and 150 outer-city white kids reverse-bussed into an innovative federally funded World of Inquiry School. At the invitation of the suburban Bannockburn PTA, 21 District of Columbia elementary school children initiated the first such exchange in the national capital area. Summer programs such as Project Wingspread in Chicago have multiplied.

But progress is slow and resistance solidifying. At least 10 suburban school boards turned down cooperation with the Hartford experiment. Law suits are underway contesting the fully paid-for presence of the D.C. children in Bannockburn. A state-ordered plan in Mount Vernon, N.Y., similar to Berkeley's, is tangled in community dissension and court litigation.

It is a struggle at the federal level, too. The Commission recommended greatly enlarging Title IV of the Civil Rights Act of 1964, which provides federal technical assistance to schools attempting desegregation. But funding remained at the $10 million level, and most of it went into the South, where despite a 14-year-old Supreme Court decision only 20 per cent of Negro students are in desegregated schools.

Title VI of the same act, which cuts off federal aid to

schools practicing discrimination, moved from South to North in October when the Department of Health, Education, and Welfare issued warnings to Union Township, N.J., and Middletown, Ohio. Since 1967, the Title VI office has been collecting racial census data from all sizable school districts, the first time such systematic data are available. Surveying about 2,000 districts for "deliberate" segregation, field investigators closed in on 38 moderate-sized cities. Changes do occur without the actual use of the cutoff club: In Pasadena, parents filed a court suit; in Wichita, the school board agreed to modify some of its policies. But the officials who have been working with these programs strongly believe that without the threat, there would be no action. President Nixon's campaign comments about using Title VI to spur desegregation caused considerable speculation that he intended a slowdown of the already barely perceptible pace of desegregation. This speculation increased when HEW Secretary Finch held up the cutoff of aid to five Southern districts, putting their funds in escrow while giving them additional time to comply. Finch, however, then did deny aid to three other districts, and said: "The law is on the books and we're going to enforce it nationally, not just in the South."

The Department of Justice similarly took belated, important first steps in enforcing the law in urban areas. Its first school desegregation suit in the North charged discrimination in faculty and student assignments in South Holland, Ill., which is now using Title IV funds to plan changes. Other suits are underway in Indianapolis; Tulsa; and East St. Louis, Ill. In each instance, a careful case has been blocked out to show the existence of discrimination above and beyond housing patterns.

In 1968, Massachusetts was added to the list of states —such as New York, California, Washington—that have laws going beyond the federal statute in condemning skewed racial populations in the schools. New Jersey will be considering such a law in early 1969. A number of law suits have been filed under these statutes, particularly by the National Association for the Advancement of Colored People, to get de facto segregation defined and declared illegal. The results are inconsistent: NAACP lost three cases in Kansas City, Kans.; Gary, Ind., and Manhasset, N.Y.; it won in Springfield, Mass.

If disillusionment plagues the goal of integration, it is no less the case with the Commission's parallel education strategy, the improvement of ghetto schools through compensatory programs. It has struck the supporters of such programs, who had overemphasized the possibilities of quick success; the economizers, who don't like spending all that money, and now a third group which says the programs won't work until students achieve a sense of destiny control in community-run schools.

The focus of this disillusionment in educational circles in 1967 was New York City's ambitious and expensive More Effective Schools program, which brought to bear a battery of the kind of innovations proposed by the Commission on selected disadvantaged schools at an average added cost of $470 per pupil. An evaluation damned the program for not closing the reading and mathematics gap, and it became something of a political (and professional) football. Late last year another evaluation decided MES was having an impact after all [24]

—but by then all eyes were on the titanic struggle over decentralization.

Also last year, the Office of Education published a compendium of 150 "outstanding" compensatory projects funded under Title I of the Elementary and Secondary Education Act, running the gamut from work-study programs, health services, remedial reading and tutoring programs, teacher education, and summer sessions to free breakfasts.[25] OE has a "Follow Through" program which attempts to sort out the approaches that work best for teaching young children. It touches on the Commission's major strategies, seeking comparative information about the benefits of curriculum change, lower pupil-teacher ratios, racial and socioeconomic mix, use of community aides, and community control. In 1968, Follow Through was expanded to include some 60 intentionally varied programs that will be evaluated for their impact on the children's achievement, self-regard, and social competence.

A related OE effort is the focusing of multiple programs on the same child. After the Detroit riots, School Superintendent Norman Drachler, in consultation with OE officials, worked out a program to concentrate a variety of program funds for the disadvantaged—medical, dental, employment, Titles I and III (special aid for innovative programs) and so on. This became a model for OE's Central Cities project, announced in 1968, to give $13 million of Title III money to 125,000 students for a "broad span of educational activities" in specific schools and neighborhoods in 26 cities. Different strategies are being used, involving early childhood education, transition to work, teacher training, and community involvement.

Title I, which has been priming disadvantaged schools with about a billion dollars annually since 1965, itself came up for evaluation of its second year of operation in 1968. The report expressed cautious optimism about what was being accomplished. Achievement levels were moving up, but not nearly enough to wipe out the gap between poor and nonpoor students. Some used the report to pronounce compensatory education a failure; others protested that the experiment was damned before it had barely begun. OE Commissioner Harold Howe II insisted that after three years of operation, the Title I efforts were beginning to pay off in real change, not just "add-ons" to more of the same.

Although Title I is a program of general aid for low-income children rather than of research, many hope to draw from the thousands of programs it underwrites some systematic objective comparison of costs and benefits. This cannot now be done. The Commission recommended that local school districts be required to make a thorough evaluation of their work as a condition of receiving Title I money. States have so far successfully fought off stronger evaluation efforts by the federal government, although some are beefing up their own evaluation capability and requirements at the state level.

The Title I appropriation was spared the Congressional paring suffered by other education programs: Funding remained about the same billion dollars a year as previously. Although hailed as a victory, this was a substantial cut from the original authorization of $2.7 billion. A billion dollars a year sounds like a healthy sum, but it comes down to $108 per assisted pupil [26] —not very much considering that it goes to schools that have been systematically underfunded and to children whose needs are overwhelming. The per-capita amount is actually declining, partly because the number of children benefiting has been going up, partly because the money is spread around to several million more children than originally intended.

The law earmarked Title I money for school districts with "concentrations of children from low-income families." Congress, however, defined this to mean any district with at least 10 poor children—qualifying such wealthy suburbs as Montgomery County, Md.; Scarsdale, N.Y.; and Shaker Heights, Ohio. The funds, moreover, can be used for such schoolwide services as guidance programs and libraries, further diluting their impact on poor children. The most recent report of the National Advisory Council on the Education of Disadvantaged Children made this judgment: "Title I funds—while spent for entirely worthy purposes—have simply failed to achieve the overall purpose of the legislation."

As recommended by the Civil Disorders Commission and others, Howe made a determined effort last year to get school districts to concentrate Title I money on fewer students so that more models of excellence could be developed. There is no clout behind the commissioner's revised "criteria," however, since the ultimate decisions about the expenditure of Title I money are made by the state and local school districts. The issue is steamy politically, since concentration in one area means withdrawal from another.

The Teacher Corps, which the Commission recommended be strengthened and expanded into a "major national program," [27] remains hampered by late and inadequate funding. It now has 2,000 young people—

two-thirds in cities—simultaneously working in inner-city schools and training in colleges. The Corps was funded at $18 million in fiscal 1968, and $20.9 million in fiscal 1969, down from an original request for $31.1 million. Applicants run about seven times the available places. This year the Ford Foundation financed about 900 applicants who had been turned down by the federal program for lack of funds.

Eventually, any realistic discussion turns back to funds. There can be no substantial improvement in the quality or equality of education for a large number of children without institutional and process change—but it will also take lots of money for leverage. The federal contribution to education—now about 8 per cent of the total—has leveled off. The trend is to block or broad grants passed through the state departments of education. Decisions on Title III grants for innovative programs were switched by Congress last year from OE to the states. Commissioner Howe took a parting shot at the states before he left office, warning that federal block grants for elementary and secondary schools should be for "national purposes which have national priorities." Said Howe, "Unless such funds find their purposes designated by Congress, they will not be used to make changes in schools in behalf of children . . . who are ill-served by the schools as they are."

There is, nevertheless, a rethinking underway of the legal and financial responsibilities of states. If education is indeed so central to curing poverty, the quality of service—or at least dollar input—can no longer be a geographical accident, producing inequities not only between one region or state and others, but between city and suburb in the same metropolitan area. As the Commission data showed, state contributions based on outdated aid formulas often accentuate the disparities. City children end up with less per capita, even though it costs more to deliver the same educational services to them than to suburban children, and they need much more.

State legislatures have tinkered a bit with the inequities. New York State set aside $26 million for aid to education in poverty areas. Maryland passed an $80 million school construction loan, the largest ever proposed. Ohio is paying school districts $100 for each child in the Aid for Dependent Children program.

In a head-on attack on the system of state aid, six cases were filed last year—in Chicago, Detroit, Los Angeles, San Antonio, Muskogee, Okla., and Bath City, W.Va.—to define "equality of educational opportunity" and pin down the state's responsibility for providing it. Some of the suits argue for equal expenditure; others that equal protection of the laws requires unequal expenditures based on the city child's extra needs.

The Chicago suit was thrown out by the U.S. District Court in November which claimed that although the state aid formula was unequal, the remedy was in the legislature, not the courts. The plaintiffs—students and parents—intend to pursue their case in the Supreme Court. A particularly strong case is being built for an upcoming suit filed by the Detroit Board of Education against the State of Michigan.

Perhaps no measure of the break in faith with the public school system is as telling as the proposals coming from all sorts of respectable people—conservative economist Milton Friedman, Henry Levin of Stanford University, Dean Theodore Sizer and Christopher Jencks of the Harvard Graduate School of Education—that parents of poor children be given public funds in the form of vouchers to "shop" for a better education in competing nonreligious private schools.

This radical (and possibly unconstitutional) idea is supported by the success of the educational programs that have sprung up outside of the "straight" school system—the street academies, the MIND program, black culture store-front schools. Although these reach only a fraction of the youngsters rejected by the schools, they demonstrate the simple truth that the same student who fails in one situation can succeed in another.

The near despair surrounding education in the slums and ghettos has had an impact, although not in terms of producing a massive solution to sever the predictability that now exists between a child's race and family income and his schooling. No one has a remedy that he can prove works. Nevertheless, the percentage of Negroes aged 25 to 29 who are high school graduates has risen to 58 in 1968, up 8 per cent from 1966. (The comparable 1968 figure for whites was 75 per cent.) The schools have introduced many changes to cope with a failure that no one even talked about less than a decade ago.

3. *Environment*

Environment in the slums and ghettos is the sum total of littered, rutted streets and a skyscape of signs and wires; of aged schools and ill-equipped, scarce playgrounds, of abandoned cars and abandoned buildings. But the environment most shaping is that of one's own dwelling place. "In nearly every disorder city surveyed," the Commission said, "grievances relating to housing were important factors in the structure of Negro discontent."

It was in 1949, the Commission recalled, that Congress established the goal of a "decent home and suitable environment for every American family." Yet "after more than three decades of fragmented and grossly under-funded federal housing programs, decent housing remains a chronic problem for the disadvantaged urban household." Nearly two-thirds of the nonwhite families in central cities, the Commission reported, "live in neighborhoods marked by substandard housing and general urban blight. For these citizens, condemned by segregation and poverty to live in the decaying slums of our central cities, the goal of a decent home and suitable environment is as far distant as ever."

Postwar housing progress has left the slums and ghettos behind, the Commission said. The nation built 16.8 million new dwelling units in the 1950's, but only

4 million were in the central cities. At the same time 1.5 million units in the cities were destroyed. The result was that, at a time of rising Negro immigration, the number of substandard units declined in the cities—but the number of nonwhites living in substandard housing increased from 1.4 to 1.8 million.

In the "disorder cities" surveyed by the Commission, 47 per cent of units occupied by nonwhites were substandard, and 24 per cent were overcrowded (against 8.8 per cent of those occupied by whites). The median rent as a proportion of median income was more than 25 per cent higher for nonwhites than for whites.

"The reasons many Negroes live in decaying slums are not difficult to discover," the Commission said: They are once again, the familiar doublet of poverty and racial discrimination. Poverty means they cannot pay rents or prices required for new or rehabilitated units, and hence are not a market for the building industry; the same factor deters landlords from investing in maintenance of existing buildings, rendering housing codes all but unenforceable. Racial discrimination "prevents access to many non-slum areas, particularly the suburbs," and creates a "back pressure" in the ghetto that increases overcrowding and boosts rents to abnormal heights.

Basic strategies

The Commission called for a two-sided effort to expand the low-income housing supply "on a massive basis": First, build more of it, specifically six million units in a five-year period; and second, "raise the rent-paying capability of low-income households." It also proposed a conscious national effort to open nonghetto areas to minority residents. "Residential segregation prevents equal access to employment opportunities and obstructs efforts to achieve integrated education," the Commission said. "A single society cannot be achieved as long as this cornerstone of segregation stands."

To achieve its construction goal, the Commission recommended vast expansion of federal mortgage subsidy, public housing, rent supplement, model cities, and urban renewal programs—maximum use of every tool at hand, with some modifications. To give low-income families access to existing housing, it recommended ending the restriction of rent supplements to new construction and making wider use of the leasing provisions of the public housing program.

"The key to breaking down housing discrimination," the Commission said, is a federal fair housing law providing "universal and uniform coverage." And federal low- and moderate-income housing programs should be aimed squarely at nonghetto areas: "Public housing programs should emphasize scattered site construction; rent supplements should, wherever possible, be used in nonghetto areas, and an intensive effort should be made to recruit [housing] sponsors willing to build outside the ghettos." Otherwise, the Commission warned, the achievement of its six-million-unit goal would be "counterproductive" in its long-range impact on society.

One year later

Two additional Presidential study groups have told the nation all it needs to know—perhaps more than it wants to know—about housing problems and programs. Out of one, the Kaiser Committee, the President drew ambitious new national housing goals (although not so ambitious as the Civil Disorders Commission's). Congress put these goals and a wide range of new programs into law, then cut back on their authorized funding. Housing construction for the poor and near-poor increased significantly, but there was not enough money behind the new national commitment to assure its achievement in the years just ahead.

The two groups who added their reports to the Civil Disorders Commission's in the Presidential archives were the National Commission on Urban Problems, headed by former Senator Paul H. Douglas, and the President's Committee on Urban Housing, directed by industrialist Edgar H. Kaiser.[28] Both contributed to a more complete picture of housing need. The Kaiser Committee, drawing on a study commissioned from TEMPO, General Electric's Advanced Studies Center, reported that one in eight American families cannot afford the market price for standard housing without paying more than 20 per cent of their total income for it. The nation's housing stock, the committee said, consists of some 66 million units, of which 2.7 million are dilapidated, 4 million without indoor plumbing, and 6.1 million overcrowded (occupied by 1.01 or more persons per room). In 1968 only 2 million standard units were vacant and on the market, the lowest vacancy rate in a decade.

The Douglas Commission focused on areas of concentrated need: "If you are poor and nonwhite and rent, the chances are three out of four that you live in substandard housing. To use another measure, 45 per cent of all nonwhite owner-household families had incomes of $3,000 or less. . . . But these poverty families occupied 72 per cent of the substandard, nonwhite owner-occupied housing." The Douglas report also drew upon a special Census Bureau study of housing in poverty areas in central cities, where it found housing density to be 100 times as great as in the suburbs. Within these poverty areas were four out of five of all housing units occupied by nonwhites in the cities and three out of four of the cities' total number of substandard dwellings.

The Kaiser Committee emphasized, however, that housing for the poor must be linked to an over-all increase in the housing production rate. Its estimate of the over-all need for the decade 1968–78 comprised 13.4 million housing units for new family formations, 8.7 million to replace dwellings that would deteriorate, 3 million to replace dwellings that would be torn down or otherwise removed, 1.6 million to allow enough vacancies for a mobile population—or a grand total of 26 million units. Six to eight million would be federally subsidized for low- and moderate-income families. The six-million goal was the same as the Civil Disorders Commission's recommendation, but the timetable was stretched from five years to ten. Housing professionals were unanimous in feeling that the Kaiser pace was more realistic. A rate of 600,000 subsidized units a year was more than ten times the average of recent years; it had taken the public housing program three decades to produce 667,000 units, according to the Douglas Commission. The Kaiser goal was adopted in the Housing Act of 1968.

The federal government approached this goal with what was, in relation to past performance, a running start. After the summer, 1967, civil disorders, the President had ordered an acceleration of public housing and related programs. The result was a 50 per cent increase in production. In fiscal 1968, 46,000 units of public housing were built and another 19,000 leased; 12,000 units were built under the rent supplement program, which had produced a total of only 3,000 units in the three previous years.[29] The new turnkey method of public housing, under which private builders put it up for guaranteed sale to public agencies, was responsible for 10,000 units of the increase.

The 1968 Act also introduced new interest-subsidy programs for both rental and sales housing for lower-income families; expanded assistance to nonprofit housing sponsors; established a new high-speed procedure for urban renewal, and put into renewal a requirement that 20 per cent of the housing built on land it provides be for low-income families; and set up "National Housing Partnerships" to encourage capital participation by private corporations in the housing effort. Authorizations for all existing programs were substantially increased in line with the new goal.

Then the appropriations machinery went to work. The same Congress that had approved the new interest-subsidy programs and authorized $75 million each to get them started in fiscal 1969 appropriated only $25 million each. Rent supplements were cut from $65 million to $30 million; model cities from $500 million to $312.5 million, and so on down the line. "Unless the new programs are funded more adequately," the Douglas Commission report commented bluntly, "the new Act cannot achieve its goals."

The Department of Housing and Urban Development estimates that there is money in the fiscal 1969 budget to build 75,000 units of public housing, 21,000 units of rent supplement housing, and, counting 47,000 units under the Farmers Home Administration, 233,000 subsidized units in all. The government will spend an estimated $2,313,000,000 for all housing and community development programs, an estimated 1.3 per cent of the total federal budget.[30] For additional budget perspective, in fiscal 1969 the federal government will spend $4.2 billion on highways.

In terms of nonfiscal substance, the 1968 Act went beyond the Civil Disorders Commission's recommendations in adding to the variety and flexibility of federal housing tools. Only one area was excepted, and that was the separation of rent supplements from new construction, a more significant exception than it might sound. A growing number of housing reformers have been suggesting that federal aids for housing construction be separated from federal aids for poor people in need of shelter; that the objectives of stimulating housing production and upgrading the environment of the poor are separate objectives requiring separate forms of subsidy. Aside from rehabilitation, only two federal housing assistance programs are not completely tied to new construction: Under recent provisions of public housing law, a local authority can lease dwelling units and sometimes buy existing buildings; and under the new interest-subsidy program for homeowners, 25 per cent of the initial money can be used to aid in purchase of existing homes.

A switch to housing allowances was rejected by the Douglas Commission, which said: "An increase in purchasing power for housing that does not, at the same time, increase materially the supply of housing available can only result in higher prices for the existing supply unless, of course, other means of increasing the available supply are in operation at the same time." The Kaiser

Committee argued for so-called "housing allowances" to the poor on an experimental basis. Its arguments were that "a housing allowance would allow a recipient family greater freedom of choice in location and type of housing; . . . would enable the free market in housing to operate in the traditional manner of supply and demand, with greater use of existing standard dwellings for housing lower-income families; . . . [and] homebuilders could respond to a new and effective demand market for standard housing units." The Committee also cautioned that a large-scale change to allowances might have an inflationary impact on the housing economy.

A housing allowance would diminish the economic barrier to the exercise of "greater freedom of choice" by residents of the decaying slums and ghettos. Another barrier would remain, that of racial prejudice. What the Commission cited as the key to its removal, a federal fair housing law, somewhat surprisingly became available in 1968.

Fair housing was made part of the Administration's Civil Rights Act of 1968, but with slim hopes that it would pass. By the time the Commission's report appeared, two attempts to cut off a filibuster on the Act had failed. A third attempt succeeded just after the report's release. The final tragic impetus to passage of the Act was the assassination of Dr. Martin Luther King: It became his legislative memorial, and was signed by the President April 11.

Two months later, the Supreme Court ruled that an 1866 statute forbade racial discrimination in the sale or rental of property. The Court noted that the Reconstruction Era law provided only for redress of private parties and was not backed "by a complete arsenal of federal authority."

Enforcement of the 1968 Act's housing provisions was put in the hands of the Department of Housing and Urban Development, and the Administration asked for $11 million to build its arsenal. The Senate voted $9 million but the House denied any appropriation at all, and prevailed in a conference committee. Later a supplementary appropriation of $2 million was voted.

The Act only gradually will become the kind of comprehensive fair housing measure advocated by the Commission. Initially, under a compromise timetable, it applied only to federally assisted housing, which amounts to 2 to 3 per cent of the total housing supply. On January 1, single-family homes in new developments and most apartment buildings came under the law, adding an estimated 43 million units. At the same time the Act's prohibition against discrimination in financing and brokerage services went into effect. In 1970, all single-family homes sold or rented by real estate agents will be included. The eventual coverage is estimated by HUD at 80 per cent of all housing units.

The 1968 Act called for HUD to "administer the programs and activities relating to housing and urban development in a manner affirmatively to further" open housing policies. This language could be interpreted (and was by some officials) as the department's first legislative mandate to positively pursue the goal of desegregation—the first step toward the Commission's recommended use of federal housing and community development programs to open alternatives to the ghetto for the minorities and poor.

"Federal programs have done little to prevent the

growth of racially segregated suburbs around our cities," the Commission report said. Until 1949, it noted, "FHA official policy was to refuse to insure any unsegregated housing." President Kennedy's "stroke of a pen" Executive Order 11063 in 1962 prohibited federal aid to any racially segregated housing or urban renewal project, but it was unevenly applied: Many cities continued to build most of their public housing in ghetto areas where segregation was inevitable.

Often the reason was that they could not find sites for it anywhere else. Public resistance to living near housing for the minorities and poor can be as formidable in the cities as in the suburbs. Consultant George Schermer detailed the impact of this resistance on the public housing program in a 1968 report for the Douglas Commission: "In city after city the local authorities were forced to abandon vacant sites outside the central slum areas because of the objections of nearby white property owners. Racial fear and prejudice were at the root of much of the opposition, but there were other reasons for it. Public housing, by its very nature, meant large aggregations of the poor in settings reminiscent of the poor farm. Middle- and working-class people did not want this kind of intrusion into their neighborhoods. . . . In many cities, compromises were made which led to debasement of the program. Often, the only sites available were in isolated, poorly developed "backwash" locations or on very expensive land in slum areas. Insofar as slum sites were used, land costs dictated the development of high-density, highrise buildings."[31]

Nor was public housing an attractive neighbor. Continues Schermer, "The entire public housing bureaucracy was governed by the necessity of demonstrating to the critics that the housing being built was bare of any amenities which might be pleasing to the eye. Nothing suggesting comfort or 'frills' could be included. It became a part of the creed that public housing was for shelter only."

The difficulty in finding sites, more than the shortage of appropriations, has been a major deterrent to construction of more public housing. The rent-supplement program has been similarly hampered. It was introduced with the stated purpose of encouraging economic mix (talk of racial mix was avoided) with subsidized and unsubsidized families living side by side in the same project. Stringent limitations on costs and amenities have been applied to rent-supplement housing, however, with the result that it is often unappealing to unsubsidized families and prospective neighbors alike. Local governments also were given a veto over its use in their communities: Any locality not wanting subsidized housing inside its borders, in fact, need only fail to adopt the so-called "workable program for community improvement" required by most federal aid programs. (Exemption of the 1968 Housing Act's interest-subsidy programs from this requirement was considered a major victory.)

As long as such obstacles stand, it will be impossible to achieve the Commission's goal of opening broad new housing choices outside of the ghettos to the minorities and the poor. And as long as this remains impossible, it will be unlikely that the 1968 Act's production goals for subsidized housing will be achieved, even with an increase in public and private investment.

These sobering facts were made evident by both the Kaiser and Douglas reports, and both offered far-reaching remedies. The Douglas Commission proposed that states be given federal encouragement to use their powers of eminent domain to open extra-ghetto sites for low- and moderate-income housing. It proposed too that state housing laws be used to give cities the right to lease housing for the poor and near-poor outside of their own boundaries. The Kaiser Committee proposed that the federal government be given power of eminent domain to acquire land anywhere to be used for subsidized housing, subject only to the state governor's veto. It also proposed federal power of preemption of local zoning ordinances, often used to exclude subsidized housing, again giving the governor a veto. The Kaiser report recommended that the workable program be dropped entirely. The Douglas report, with greater subtlety, recommended that it apply not just to subsidized housing and renewal but to more popular programs such as water and sewer grants.

No widespread support for such proposals is evident in Congress. It will take time to convert federal housing programs into tools for opening new choices, and meanwhile millions live, willingly or unwillingly, in the shabby environment of the slums and ghettos. Progress there is painstaking and increasingly complicated. Rehabilitation of slum dwellings, advanced for a time as a panacea, has been slowed by tight money and its own inherent diseconomies of scale: In fiscal 1968, only 8,000 units were rehabilitated under the major federal loan and grant programs, and the fiscal 1969 estimate is 16,000. (Hope that technology would unblock rehabilitation declined with a 1968 report on the widely publicized "instant rehab" project in New York City, in which whole cores were dropped into apartments and they were thoroughly refurbished in 48 hours. The report, by the Institute for Public Administration, found the experiment too expensive to be replicated.[32]

Urban renewal, increasingly turned into a tool to help low-income families, continued at an annual expenditure level of $800 million. Another $412.5 million in renewal funds were earmarked for use in the model cities program, which continued to show the promise held out for it in the Commission report. Since the inception of the model cities program in November, 1967, 150 communities have received grants to plan the physical and social reconstruction of slums and ghettos. Early this year the first actual program funds were disbursed to nine cities, and there were indications that the new Administration found in the model cities program a concept worth expanding. Tough citizen participation requirements had been built into model cities. In some communities they were seriously delaying the program; in a few they were resulting in a kind of progress more significant than bricks and mortar. In model cities there was the hope, if a hope limited by appropriations, of finding the means to reduce the destructiveness of the slum-ghetto environment.

4. Conclusions

"It is time now to turn with all the purpose at our command to the major unfinished business of this nation," the Commission said a year ago. It called on the nation "to mount programs on a scale equal to the dimension of the problems; to aim these programs for high impact in the immediate future in order to close the gap between promise and performance; to undertake new initiatives and experiments that can change the system of failure and frustration that now dominates the ghetto and weakens our society." The following summarizes the nation's response in relation to the elements of the system examined in the preceding pages.

Poverty

1. Employment and income have risen in the slum-ghetto in both absolute and relative terms. Poverty remains a pervasive fact of life there, however, and the continuing disparity between this poverty and the general affluence remains a source of alienation and discontent.

2. Further gains in employment and income in the slums and ghettos are dependent on continued prosperity. But prosperity alone will not upgrade the hard-core poor and unemployed. Specific programs are necessary to meet their special needs and problems.

3. The largest gap in these programs, as they affect employment, is lack of a public job-creation program to complement increased public-private job-training efforts.

4. Job discrimination remains a serious problem, reinforcing the concentration of minorities in low-pay, low-status occupations.

5. Increased attention has been given efforts to open business opportunities to minorities, but only limited progress has been made.

6. No progress has been made in reform of the welfare system. Judicial gains have been offset by the threat of backward steps posed by the 1967 amendments to federal welfare laws.

7. Development and public acceptance of an income-supplementation system is still not in sight.

Education

1. The major issue to emerge in the past year is that of decentralization or community control of schools. Its impact on the quality of slum-ghetto education cannot yet be evaluated.

2. Despite a turning away of some blacks from school integration as a goal, it has been pursued with some success in small- to moderate-size cities. There is no evidence of success in big cities with substantial minority populations.

3. Federal enforcement of laws and judicial rulings against school segregation has been of limited effectiveness in the South and is only beginning in the North.

4. Direct efforts to improve ghetto schools through compensatory programs are hampered by shortages of funds and by lack of means to measure precisely their

effectiveness. Federal aid each year is spread more thinly and state aid is inequitably distributed.

5. Ghetto schools continue to fail. The small amount of progress that has been made has been counterbalanced by a growing atmosphere of hostility and conflict in many cities.

Environment

1. Two Presidential study groups have expanded and made more precise the nation's knowledge about housing need and how to meet it. Out of their work has come Congressional commitment to a well-documented housing production goal.

2. The Housing Act of 1968 substantially expanded the programmatic tools necessary to meet this goal. But appropriations cuts pushed its attainment far into the future.

3. Passage of a federal fair housing law represented the first essential step for opening new housing choices to residents of the slums and ghettos. Its impact will be hampered by inadequate appropriations for enforcement.

4. There are as yet no sufficient means to direct federal housing and community improvement programs toward opening extra-ghetto areas to the poor and minorities. In their absence, problems of finding acceptable sites also are likely to hamper seriously realization of the 1968 act's goal for construction of subsidized housing.

5. Rehabilitation has not fulfilled its promise as a means of improving the slum-ghetto environment. The model cities program, using a redirected approach to urban renewal, continues to offer promise limited only by its level of funding. At present, however, there are no

programs that seriously threaten the continued existence of the slums.

Progress in dealing with the conditions of slum-ghetto life has been nowhere near in scale with the problems. Nor has the past year seen even a serious start toward the changes in national priorities, programs, and institutions advocated by the Commission. The sense of urgency in the Commission report has not been reflected in the nation's response.

PART II

One Society or Two?

Other groups have lived in poverty, in slums. They escaped. Their descendants now ask why the Negroes can't make it too without "handouts," without riots.

The Commission devoted an entire chapter to the answer. The earlier immigrants didn't make it all that easily or quickly; they were admitted to the political system, gained jobs and favors from it that reform has largely eliminated; there were more opportunities for unskilled workers then.

But the largest factor cited by the Commission was race. Damaged by a history that went from slavery to slums, the Negro continues to be blocked by a "structure of discrimination" beyond anything the earlier immigrants had encountered.

The Commission was relentless in its emphasis on race. The headline phrase was "white racism," taken out of Chapter 4, an indictment that was widely resented. It devoted another chapter to describing the impact of racism on the Negro from the time he set foot in America, a chained foot.

"What white Americans have never fully understood —but what the Negro can never forget—is that white society is deeply implicated in the ghetto," it said. "White institutions created it, white institutions maintain it, and white society condones it."

What the Commission called its "basic conclusion" had to do with race: "Our nation is moving toward two societies, one black, one white—separate and unequal." What was, in reality, its basic recommendation—at once more fundamental and more radical than suggestions of institutional change or ghetto improvement—was that society make itself one.

The Commission took the nation systematically through three choices available to it. The first was to continue "present policies," which the Commission said were not sufficient to change "the key factors of Negro concentration, racial segregation, and the lack of sufficient enrichment to arrest the decay of deprived neighborhoods."

The second choice it called "enrichment," under which enough resources would be applied "to make a dramatic, visible impact on life in the urban Negro ghetto." Nothing would be done to lessen Negro concentration. The Commission argues, essentially, that separate can never be equal in any area of ghetto life. "The economy of the United States and particularly the sources of employment are preponderantly white"; separatism "could only relegate Negroes permanently to inferior incomes and economic status." The enrichment choice is "essentially another way of choosing a permanently divided country."

The third choice is to combine ghetto enrichment with "programs designed to encourage integration of substantial numbers of Negroes into the society outside the ghetto." The goal, the Commission said, "must be achieving freedom for every citizen to live and work according to his capacities and desires, not his color." In addition to the worthiness of this goal, the Commission pointed out that integration would have the practical effects of allowing the urban employed to live out where the jobs increasingly are, would improve the education of children now in the ghetto, and would facilitate construction of more low- and moderate-income housing.

Even at the time the Commission report was being prepared, integration was coming into disfavor as a word and as a goal. In several cities struck by disorders, the Commission said in its discussion of the aftermath, "increasing polarization is evident, with continuing breakdown of interracial communication, and growth of white segregationist or black separatist groups." In the nation as a whole, it found that "reaction to last summer's disorders has quickened the movement [toward two societies] and deepened the division" between black and white.

The following pages examine the past year for evidence of whether the nation is closer to being one society or two.

5. Violence and Response, 1968

It was a year in which the heat and turbulence of past urban summers arrived in spring. Martin Luther King was killed on April 4, and in the ensuing seven days 203 civil disorders broke out, according to Brandeis University's Lemberg Center for the Study of Violence. By the end of the month there had been 237 (202 "definite" and 35 "equivocal" by the center's measurement) of which 47 involved fatalities and/or property damage over $1,000. The center's total of disorders for the entire year of 1967 was 249. In its progress report to the President, the Commission on the Causes and Prevention of Violence said of April: "This was the first time—and the only time to date—that disorders in different cities have been touched off by a single national event."

Summer was quieter. Still, by August the number of 1968 civil disorders had increased 194 per cent over 1967, according to the International City Managers' Association.[33] The association used a more exacting definition of civil disorders than the Lemberg Center: Its total for 1967 was 82, and for January–August, 1968, 241. Its survey nevertheless showed that 44 per cent of the central cities in the United States experienced civil disorder between January, 1967, and August, 1968.

By the association's reckoning, civil disorders lasted

509 aggregate days of the seven months of 1968 against 283 days in 1967; there were 29,214 arrests against 17,306 in 1967, 4,313 injuries against 3,808, and 69 deaths against 84. The last was the only figure to show a reduction.

It was a significant figure, because it reflected the changed nature of response to civil disorder. After summer, 1967, the press was filled with news of cities equipping themselves with everything from chemical spray to heavy armor in preparation for what one author called "The Second Civil War." What was actually happening was a sophisticated re-examination of the civic response to civil disorder, instigated by the Commission itself. The following summary draws from an unpublished and unedited manuscript prepared by Jack Rosenthal, national urban affairs correspondent of *Life* magazine (and principal editor of the Commission report), for the Twentieth Century Fund project on "The Military Establishment and American Life."

In October, 1967, early in its investigations, the Commission determined that (1) some cities had developed considerable expertise in riot control and prevention, and (2) that most cities were unaware of their techniques. The Commission recommended to the President that a series of conferences be called to spread this knowledge, and the President instructed Attorney General Ramsey Clark to do so.

In winter of 1967–68, some 400 mayors, city managers, and police officials from the 136 largest cities in the country attended four one-week sessions at Airlie House, a conference center near Washington. They were sponsored jointly by the Department of Justice and the International Association of Chiefs of Police. Says Rosenthal of these conferences, "Quinn Tamm, director of the International Association of Chiefs of Police, suggests that they were decisive in shaping understanding of disorder prevention and control—recognition that the important questions are not so much tactics, like whether to use V-wedge riot formations, but community relations, close command supervision, and the capacity to respond to incipient disorder quickly."

The military also was taking action. After the Detroit riot of 1967, three special military boards were convened to investigate the 400,000-member National Guard's capacity to handle civil disorders, and also its low proportion of Negroes. Last year the Guard concentrated on Negro recruitment while thinning its ranks for greater effectiveness. The April disorders, when 34,900 Guardsmen were used in 22 communities, were a measure of the improvement in performance. While the Commission criticized the Guard for extensive and indiscriminate firing in summer, 1967, last April the 15,000 Guard and federal troops in Washington fired at most 15 bullets.

Of the 260,000 Army reservists in the nation, 204,000 have now received training in civil disturbances. Regular and reserve personnel, together with civil law enforcement officers, go through 40 hours of training at the Senior Officers Civil Disturbance Orientation Course at Fort Gordon, Ga. Says Rosenthal, "The curriculum ranges from community relations to arson; the dominant themes are minimum force and maximum planning."

Rosenthal credits the police and military with "considerable skill" in handling the April disorders. "We didn't shoot and they didn't shoot," a policeman told the *Washington Post*. "With all the guns that we know the people have out there and with all the guns that we have, I believe a miracle has occurred." The International Association of Chiefs of Police in August completed an eight-city survey of the April response, interviewing 16 officers of all ranks. "Not only did police personnel understand their department's policy regarding the use of fatal force," the association concluded, "but all but two of the officers interviewed agreed that it was satisfactory and would not recommend any change in future disorders."

Six of the eight cities had established riot-control detachments, capable of quick response action. "One of the traditional principles of disorder control is the rapid deployment of significant numbers of trained and equipped police," the association report said. "The recent [April] riots once again verified the basic soundness of this principle." Attorney General Clark put it another way in an interview with Rosenthal: "I would rather have 500 men in half an hour than 5,000 men in six or eight hours."

There is no question that the summer of 1968 was a relatively cool one in terms of the intensity of disorder. In June, July, and August, the National Guard was called out six times compared with 18 in the same months of 1967; there were 19 deaths compared with 87 a year earlier. Rosenthal couples these facts with the decreased likelihood of police "to incite disorder through unwitting conduct" and the increased capability of police to control disorder should it erupt: the art of "suppression without repression." On the other hand, he warns, the decline in summer disorder "may reflect only the temporary, premature exhaustions of the energies of protestors."

The International City Managers' Association analysis is more sanguine. "City administrations and police departments have become more adept at handling potential riot situations," it says. "While riot potential was greater in 1968 than in 1967, the triggering events were rapidly controlled and large-scale disorders thus were avoided."

Others also credited the restraint of the news media in preventing the escalation of disorder. When the April violence erupted, the media in many cities exercised voluntary restraint during volatile early hours. In Washington, on the night the disorders started, the first televised indication that anything was happening was the appearance of an almost tearful black city councilman (the Rev. Walter Fauntroy, a close associate of Martin Luther King) asking residents to stay in their homes.

One of the summer, 1968, disorders was ominously unlike those that had gone before. Just after 8 p.m. on the night of July 29, a police tow truck, called to the Glenville area of Cleveland to pick up an abandoned car, came under sniper fire from two sides. More police and National Guardsmen were summoned and a small war raged on the street for three hours. Three policemen were killed and so were three members of a black nationalist group alleged to have planned the ambush. Two other Negroes died in the crossfire; a third was found dead behind an empty black nationalist headquarters. Later that night a Negro marine in civilian clothes was shot and killed by whites five miles from the Glenville battleground; early the next morning a Negro folk singer driving through a white neighborhood was shot and killed when he stopped for a traffic light. Looting and arson went on sporadically for two nights in Cleveland and there were ripples of violence elsewhere: Firebombs struck a firehouse in Erie, Pa.; a group of whites were beaten by Negroes in Grand Rapids, Mich. There were alleged sniping incidents in New York and other cities in subsequent weeks. Ohio National Guard intelligence officers said a black nationalist group had scheduled Glenville-type violence for seven other Ohio cities, Pittsburgh, Chicago, and Detroit. Attorney General Clark said there was no evidence of such a widespread conspiracy.

The Cleveland battle was officially labeled an "insurrection." As the Commission on the Causes and Prevention of Violence pointed out, to many it raised "the spectre of interracial, person-oriented rioting of the kind that wracked East St. Louis in 1917, Chicago in 1919, and Detroit in 1943." But by the end of 1968, it had not happened again.

Civil disorder took at least one new and troubling turn in the past year, however. Its nature was indicated by the Commission on the Causes and Prevention of Violence.[34] "The key to much of the violence in our society seems to lie with the young," said its progress report. "Our youth account for an ever-increasing percentage of crime, greater than their increasing percentage of the population. The thrust of much of the group protest and collective violence—on the campus, in the ghettos, in the streets—is provided by our young people. It may be here, with tomorrow's generation, that much of the emphasis of our studies and the national response should lie."

The Civil Disorders Commission had concentrated on turbulence in the ghetto. The Violence Commission saw a linkage to turbulence on the campus. Until a few years ago, it said, "the extremely small minority of black students tended to be individualistic and on most campuses politically inactive. The Black Power movement, however, coupled with substantial increases in the number of black students, has offered some black students a vehicle for giving collective expression of their particular grievances and at the same time to identify them with the larger black community."

The Violence Commission suggested that "the militant stance of some black students may be a major factor in increasing the militance of white students, whose commitments to racial justice and equality have been greeted with skepticism by blacks. At Columbia, for example, the white student seizure of some campus buildings may have resulted in part from overtly expressed doubts by black students that the whites were really prepared to do what both groups felt was necessary to challenge the university and resist the police."

Since Columbia, campus conflicts at San Francisco State College, University of California at Berkeley, University of Wisconsin, Duke University, Brandeis, and elsewhere have had a distinctly racial cast; the black student movement has become the cutting edge of the black protest movement. What is most notable in the past year, however, is the extension of both from the college campus and the street to the high schools.

Student grievances and disorders are not new to urban high schools. But the kind of spreading collective action by the young who demand change is—strikes, marches, lists of demands, the seizing of principals' offices and cafeterias—and especially the spill-over into violence: scuffling between teachers and students, property destruction, arson. The Lemberg Center for the Study of Violence said 44 per cent of the April disorders were related to the schools.[35] The "overwhelming number" of these were linked to the King assassination—by demands for special memorials, the lowering of flags, and the closing of schools, and, in response, what the center calls "a certain insensitivity on the part of school officials."

At the same time, the center noted that many of the disorders were not so linked. It concluded that "unrest in the schools appears to be a general and long-range phenomenon" caused by young people's search for excitement, specific educational grievances, and "rising antagonism between white and black students."

The center has been borne out. Although no official count of school disorders is available, close observers say the problem is "universal," involving some black or integrated schools in every large city, and in smaller cities and rural areas as well.

Although each situation is different, there is also a kind of triggering pattern. The black students, usually organized as such, present a list of demands: black history, more black teachers, more participation in student affairs. They complain of overcrowding, beatings. In Boston, they demanded to wear dashikis; in Los Angeles they supported demands for community control. Escalation is part of the pattern too.

School officials have been unprepared, unable to understand what is going on, fearful, and apparently seldom willing to mediate legitimate demands lest the situation deteriorate further. Police have been called in, sometimes stationed at the schools, and mass arrests made. Schools have been closed down—in Boston, for months. The Justice Department's Community Relations Service has sent its people into schools in 19 cities.

In September, 1968, Mark A. Chesler and Ann Arbor's Center for the Utilization of Scientific Knowledge brought together school administrators and civil rights and community action experts to talk over "crisis intervention in the schools." Chesler, working under a $180,000 Ford Foundation grant in 12 cities suffering from serious student outbreaks, believes that the racial tensions in these disorders have been overplayed, that the basic problem is a clash between generations which takes on more serious overtones because the protesting school population is black and the establishment group of teachers or students white. Calling it racial gives officials an "easy out," says Chesler, to avoid dealing with the need for change in the old order. "The principals think the kids want control. They don't," says Chesler, "but they do want to influence the way the schools are run."

Others, using words like "insurrection" and "rebellion," believe the disorders are fundamentally racial. They see in the troubled schools a new manifestation of growing black-white polarization.

6. Crime and Community

Civil disorder has not simply erupted unexpectedly from a neighborhood that is placid one hour and in flames the next, the Commission pointed out. Instead, disorder "developed out of an increasingly disturbed social atmosphere, in which typically a series of tension-heightening incidents over a period of weeks or months became linked in the minds of many in the Negro community with a shared reservoir of underlying grievances." The relationship between the incidents and the grievances was complex: "For example, grievances about allegedly abusive police practices, unemployment and underemployment, housing, and other conditions in the ghetto were often aggravated in the minds of many Negroes by incidents involving the police, or the inaction of municipal authorities on Negro complaints. . . ."

One of the prime contributors to the "disturbed social atmosphere" of the slums and ghettos is crime, which, by the end of 1968, had become a national preoccupation. A Louis Harris poll in September showed that 81 per cent of the public believed that "law and order has broken down in this country." Fifty-four per cent of the respondents said "they personally feel more uneasy on the streets" and 53 per cent linked their uneasiness to "fear of racial violence." The most uneasy were residents of big cities and their suburbs in the East and South, older people, women, and Negroes.

There was ample reason for concern. In the years 1960–67, the FBI index showed crime to have risen 88 per cent, nine times the percentile increase in population. In the first eight months of 1968, the rate of increase intensified.[36] Violent crimes increased 21 per cent over the same period of 1967: murder 15 per cent, rape 17 per cent, robbery 32 per cent, aggravated assault 13 per cent. Street robbery increased 37 per cent. Some of the increase in the 1960's could be explained by better reporting procedures; some, by shifts of population from rural to urban areas where crime is more likely to come to the attention of police. But the nation clearly was in the grip of a crime epidemic.

The first major federal response came in 1968 with passage of the Safe Streets Act, providing $100 million in fiscal 1969 and $300 million in fiscal 1970 for states and localities to use in fighting crime. The funds will be disbursed in the form of block grants to the states, despite Administration objections. They can be used for preparation of state law enforcement plans, required by the Act; for a variety of law enforcement programs within these plans; and for training and research. The Act established a three-man Law Enforcement Assistance Administration in the Justice Department to administer the grants.

Crime, like other forms of social disorganization, is concentrated in the slums and ghettos of the city, the Commission pointed out. It cited a 1965 survey of five Chicago police districts which showed that a low-income Negro district had 35 times as many serious crimes as a high-income white district. Most ghetto crimes "are committed by a small minority of the residents, and the principal victims are the residents themselves," the Commission said. The probability of being robbed is 3.5 times higher for nonwhites than whites; the probability of being raped is 3.7 times higher for a nonwhite woman than a white. Crime "creates an atmosphere of insecurity and fear throughout Negro neighborhoods," and can be expected to grow faster there than elsewhere. By 1975 the number of Negroes 14 to 24 years in age will have increased by two-thirds in nine years, and it is this age group—increasingly its youngest segments—which commits most violent crimes.

The Commission concentrated its call for reform on two elements of the criminal justice system: the courts and the police. "Partially paralyzed by decades of neglect, deficient in facilities, procedures and personnel, overwhelmed by the demands of normal operations, lower courts have staggered under the crushing new burdens of civil disorders," the Commission said. They continue to stagger as crime increases. In respect to the courts, in the view of a Justice Department official, "the significant thing about the last year is that nothing can be pointed to." Trial delay at the time of writing the President's Crime Commission report of 1967 averaged eight months; by the end of 1968 it was 10½ months. Bank robberies have become almost everyday occurrences in the District of Columbia, increasing fourfold in the past year. In 1968 arrests were made in 60 of the 100 Washington bank robberies—and by year's end only one of those arrested had come to trial.[37]

But it was to the police that the Civil Disorders Commission assigned the most critical role. Half of the "precipitating incidents" of the 1967 disorders involved the police, and police practices led the Commission's list of Negro grievances in disorder cities. "To some Negroes, police have come to symbolize white power, white racism, and white repression. And the fact is that many police do reflect and express these white attitudes," the Commission said. "The atmosphere of hostility and cynicism is reinforced by a widespread belief among Negroes in the existence of police brutality and in a 'double standard' of justice and protection—one for Negroes and one for whites."

Most of the Commission's recommendations on the police were taken, with due acknowledgment, from the President's Crime Commission, which found the police to be underpaid, undereducated, undertrained, poorly selected, and too often racially prejudiced. The Civil Disorders Commission concentrated on recommendations for more Negro police, improved protection and reformed practices in the slums and ghettos, and more attention to police-community relations. It called community relations "an integral part of all law enforcement," which must include "the development of an attitude, a tone, throughout the force that conforms with the ultimate responsibility of every policeman: public service." It recommended establishing grievance mechanisms "external" to the police department, but having jurisdiction over other city departments as well as police.

No major city has installed an external police review board in the year since the Commission's report. The International Association of Chiefs of Police, whose constructive work has gone beyond riot response to a variety of programs encouraging police professionalism, draws the line at "outside" review boards: They only "aggravate the situation," a spokesman says. IACP believes police should police their own ranks, and points to Cincinnati, which published a booklet telling citizens whom to call with complaints, and Chicago, where the Patrolmen's Benevolent Association purged itself of a right-wing group, as evidence of increased internal strictness.

IACP also conducted a survey last August on the proportion of black policemen in 500 cities. In cities over a half million population, Negroes accounted for 6.6 per cent of the police forces, and the proportion declined with the size of the cities surveyed. Even in the larger cities, however, it was less than a third of the percentage of Negro residents. Major efforts at black recruitment were made by some police forces in the past year. Washington, D.C., by early 1969, had raised the percentage of blacks among its recruits from a third of the training class to a half; Detroit, in 1968, doubled the number of blacks among those hired for the force. But even IACP did not point to these as examples of a nationwide upward trend of significance.

The Ford Foundation has funded a New York City effort to recruit Negroes and Puerto Ricans returning from Viet Nam, and another to train 150 men 19 to 28 years of age from disadvantaged areas, most of them Negroes. Morgan Guaranty Trust Company has contributed $10,000 to the training program. Also in New York, in one of several experiments sponsored by the Vera Institute of Justice, 46 black and Puerto Rican youths patrolled unarmed the streets of Central Harlem's 28th Precinct for a week in March, 1968, as the Community Service Patrol Corps. Both the community and the corpsmen were enthusiastic about the results, Vera reports, and funding now is being sought to establish a two-year community corps involving up to 100 men.

An ambitious experiment in police-community co-operation is getting underway in troubled Washington, where tensions over police shootings have brought demands by the city's Black United Front for community control of the force. The Office of Economic Opportunity has given Washington $1.4 million for an 18-month effort to turn the 13th Precinct into a "model precinct." Half of the OEO funds will go for in-service police training and half to pay community residents to do full-time jobs now handled by uniformed men such as traffic control and clerical work. Some of the community employees also will staff storefront centers and a youth patrol.

Part of the experiment will be an attempt to change promotion procedures, which at present place heavy weight on such factors as numbers of arrests. William Kopit, OEO project officer for the model precinct, said there would be more emphasis on positive things "like delivering babies, rescuing children—the things policemen already spend a lot of time on, but now have to feel embarrassed about, at least as far as the force is concerned."

Negative attitudes on the force were identified by the Commission as the major obstacle to more effective police-community relations programs. It has been generally accepted in recent years that such programs are "good things" to have, but in most cases they have more to do with public relations than community relations, the Commission pointed out. There is little evidence of change in this emphasis on the part of most police departments. Kopit traveled to 10 cities during development of the model precinct plans, and found scant enthusiasm among police for community relations programs. "The police generally think they've got the public on their side," he said, "so why bother?"

The police are right about the public: The Harris Poll respondents were 87 per cent in favor of the proposition that "law and order would improve if more people backed up their local police." But there were worrisome indications in the past year that the police were moving further toward an "our side–their side" mentality and seeing their role as something more than public service.

There was, first, the growing trend toward unionization of police along with other public servants and the growing power of those departments already organized. The AFL-CIO reportedly has been moving toward nationwide unions of police and other public employees. Police and firemen have gone out on strike in Detroit, Kansas City, and Youngstown in the past two years. New York City in 1968 granted a pay raise that it thought had averted a strike, but the members of the Patrolmen's Benevolent Association weren't as pleased with the raise as their leaders. Suddenly the police force was hit with an epidemic of influenza (some policemen called it the "blue flu"); policemen who did return to duty stopped issuing parking and speeding tickets; the city had to go to court to end the slowdown. Detroit police won a substantial raise by using similar tactics.

A strike against government, labor editor A. H. Raskin wrote in the December *Saturday Review,* "becomes a political as well as an economic weapon." Raskin noted that the Fraternal Order of Police reportedly had considered a two-day national walkout to dramatize "the need for more public support of law enforcers." This kind of question, Raskin said, "should not be resolved under the gun of a strike."

An official of the International Association of Chiefs of Police found a trend toward "police militancy." The police see at close hand the tactics of students, Negroes, and other protestors, and they see that these tactics work: "Now they want a piece of the action too." In Newark police picketing forced Mayor Hugh Addonizio to back down on his blanket support of the report of the New Jersey State Select Commission on Civil Disorder, and make an exception of the Commission's recommendation of a civilian review board. In Boston, organized police resistance moved Mayor Kevin White to remove a community-relations unit from the Boston model cities application.

The increased professionalism of the police response to civil disorder contrasted with the events in Chicago during the Democratic National Convention, when, according to the Walker Commission's report on those events, the police got out of control to the point where they became the rioters. Herbert Mitgang, writing in *The New York Times* in December, said the police "are not a breed apart but an embodiment of the attitudes of a part of lower-middle-class Americans. They have their pride, their confusions about the breakdown in youth discipline, their racial prejudices, their resentment against those who call them names when the attacks are directed against institutions and government." If control and restraint weaken, if the police should become the instrument of a single class and its values rather than the community as a whole, then the "deep hostility" found by the Civil Disorders Commission between police and slum-ghetto residents can only intensify.

It is axiomatic, the Commission said, that "effective law enforcement requires the support of the community. Such support will not be present when a substantial segment of the community feels threatened by the police and regards the police as an occupying force."

7. *City Hall and the Ghetto*

Most citizens of metropolitan areas, the Commission observed, become aware of inner-city problems only when they read their tax bills or headlines about crime and riots. But there are two groups who live constantly with these problems: "the public officials and the poor, particularly the residents of the racial ghetto." The relationship between these two, the Commission said, "is a key factor in the development of conditions underlying civil disorders."

Every one of the 1967 disorders, it continued, "was foreshadowed by an accumulation of unresolved grievances by ghetto residents against local authorities," often —but by no means always—the police. The Commission found "a widening gulf in communications" between city hall and the ghetto which produces in many Negroes "a profound sense of isolation and alienation from the processes and programs of government." Other citizens feel this alienation too, but "it is far more difficult to overcome for low-income, less educated citizens who are disproportionately supported by and dependent upon programs administered by agencies of local government."

Even when local officials overcome the gulf and learn

the needs of ghetto residents, "many city governments are poorly organized to respond effectively," the Commission found. It is left to the people with the problems to make them "fit the complicated structure of government."

Finally, the Commission said that ghetto residents "increasingly believe that they are excluded from the decision-making process which affects their lives and community." Negroes are still not admitted to the political system in proportion to their numbers. The ghetto's needs for welfare and other public services have "swelled dramatically" while the needs for the majority population have diminished, so the ghetto has few natural political allies. Reform "has eliminated an important political link between city government and low-income residents"; the ward bosses are largely gone or no longer powerful enough to deliver favors or redress. In summary, the Commission offered a warning: "No democratic society can long endure the existence within its major urban centers of a substantial number of citizens who feel deeply aggrieved as a group, yet lack confidence in the government to rectify perceived injustice and in their ability to bring about needed change."

The Commission also offered a specific set of inventions to improve the situation. As a beginning, it proposed establishment of "neighborhood action task forces" which would be creatures of both the local government and the ghetto community. The task forces, including representatives of the mayor and city service agencies, would function as an interagency coordinating device and a "community cabinet," listening to and acting on community needs. Eventually, the Commission suggested, these task forces should be transformed into "neighborhood city halls" as part of the permanent structure of local government, with one-stop neighborhood centers for the coordinated delivery of services. The Commission also made some less specific recommendations about admittance of Negroes to the political system and about leadership. It assigned a formidable task to the big-city mayor: "His goal, in effect, must be to develop a new working concept of democracy within the city."

A year later, there is probably no mayor of any city of reasonable size who is not more aware of the needs and problems of the slums and ghettos, certainly none in the cities which experienced civil disorder last spring and summer. Communications have increased between city hall and the ghetto, which is not to say that the results are universally positive. Structural change is rare. Still, a new concept of local democracy is being worked out in many cities, mainly through the slow and often painful tugs-of-war of democratic politics. Gradually the ghetto residents and their spokesmen are becoming participants in the tug-of-war along with other interest groups, some of which resist their presence.

More than one big-city mayor is known to feel that the Commission's specific structural remedies, such as the task forces, were naive. Others reacted to the report by saying they were communicating all along, and of course they would continue to look for ways to make further progress. A relative few used the report as a measuring stick of progress. The International City Managers' Association surveyed its members and reported on the response of 12, all of whose cities had experienced civil disorders. Through their responses ran words such as redirection, impetus, stimulus, reordering priorities, but some insisted they had been aware of the problems identified by the Commission all along and that its report had been too harsh on the cities.

Perhaps the most specific use of the report was made in Atlanta, where Mayor Ivan Allen made it required reading for his top staff, and formed an Atlanta Advisory Committee on Civil Disorders to be sure action would follow. Government-community task forces were set up in six problem neighborhoods, and as needed could call on a citywide task force of officials from the housing authority, the schools, the fire and police departments, the building inspectors' office, and other key agencies. The mayor directed the Community Relations Commission to hold grievance hearings in the neighborhoods and report to him.

Significantly, Atlanta backed the effort in its budget. A total of $62,000 went to hire four community services officers who attend neighborhood meetings, hear complaints, and attempt to identify and get action on problems before they mount; $90,000 was provided for police-community relations officers; $300,000 was used for summer recreation programs.

Most important, in the opinion of Dan Sweat, who coordinated the program in the mayor's office, is making sure the city can deliver. Sweat personally got commitments from city agencies that they would respond—and pointed out that they could benefit from better communication with the neighborhoods. The task forces no longer meet: Sweat feels they served their purposes—airing complaints, finding out who speaks for whom on both the government and community sides of the table. The community services officers are stationed in neighborhood centers. "Citizens now know where to go for what, and we know who to go to in the neighborhoods," says Sweat.

It is hard to know which way the cause-effect relationship goes between New York City's efforts and the Commission report, since Mayor John V. Lindsay was the Commission's vice chairman. Early in his administration, Mayor Lindsay proposed a system of neighborhood city halls. The mayor is a Republican and the city council majority Democratic; city funds were refused on grounds that the neighborhood city halls might become his "clubhouses." He has persisted with private contributions, including foundation grants. There are now five neighborhood "action centers" staffed with three to 10 specially trained volunteers, each on an around-the-clock basis providing advice, referral, and access to officials who can solve problems. Their operation has been studied by representatives of some 55 cities.

New York also has established 20 "urban task forces" of city officials who work in their spare time to get close to community groups and problems. Each has a storefront office staffed by two community residents, for which the city council did approve $300,000. When tension rises, the task force members become troubleshooters: They know who the key people are in the neighborhoods and also how to cut red tape in city hall. Task force chairmen meet with the mayor every week, and use his presence in a neighborhood as the ultimate weapon when trouble comes.

The task forces were started in black and Puerto Rican communities, but this year their number will be doubled and many will operate in white neighborhoods. White resentment at "special attention" to minorities has risen steadily during the past year in New York and other cities. In New York it was fanned by the ugly charges of white racism and black anti-Semitism that were made during the school decentralization fight. The Lindsay administration is trying now to heal some of the deep hostilities that the school controversy revealed.

A similar attempt is being made in Boston by Mayor Kevin White, who has used the Lindsay technique of walking the streets to symbolize the government's concern with people. In ethnically conscious Boston, where blacks number only 85,000 of a total population of 617,000, Mayor White has not confined his walks to the ghettos: He also can be found shooting basketball in Irish Charlestown or inspecting a run-down school in Italian East Boston.

Mayor White has created an Office of Public Service which includes a city hall information center, open to letters and telephone calls 24 hours a day, and little city halls set up with municipal funds. There are 10 of these outposts called "neighborhood service centers," and the mayor hopes to add three more in spring. Most are in portable trailers that cost $5,000 to buy and furnish. They handle an average of 900 complaints a week. Most of their managers do not live in the neighborhoods they serve, a result of political prudence: If they do their jobs well, they could become powerful political forces out of neighborhood loyalty.

Mayor White has had to defend the neighborhood city halls repeatedly from jealousy on the part of local officeholders and officials of city agencies. In its annual report on 1968, the Advisory Commission on Intergovernmental Relations notes that the drive to decentralize the structure of city government has been met with "varying degrees of cynicism, alarm, and vigorous opposition by political leaders and municipal administrators. A number

. . . fear these developments might further clutter the already fragmented local government landscape." On the other hand, it finds that "civil rights militants, poverty workers, and other advocates of closer, more personal government" feel that steps such as neighborhood city halls don't go nearly far enough.[38]

Agreement for the latter view came in a paper presented to the American Political Science Association by Gary T. Marx of Harvard University in September. While Marx was critical of the Commission report, his assessment of how cities had responded to civil disorder was similar to the Commission's: some change but not enough. Steps such as "the repeal of an anti-loitering law, the appointment of a black precinct captain or special assistant to the mayor, the release of anti-poverty funds, the creation of a few new jobs, the enforcement of housing codes, the improvement of garbage collection, and the provision of portable swimming pools, do not change the face of modern America," Marx wrote, though acknowledging that "in some small degree they may make life more tolerable for many of those victimized by intolerance and indifference."

Marx built a matrix of the cities he surveyed based on the extent of disorder, categories of grievances, and the racial sensitivity of local officials before disorder occurred. He put them into three categories: In Atlanta; Grand Rapids, Mich.; and New Brunswick, N.J., he found cities with already responsive administrations where civil disorders were followed by positive changes and no noticeable increase in polarization between the races. In Detroit, Cincinnati, and Plainfield, N.J., there had been both positive change and increased polarization after major disorders. In cities which he described as "conservative" in racial policies—Cambridge, Md.; Waukegan, Ill.; Jersey City—small to medium disorders had been followed by increased polarization and no change for the better.[39]

Faced with this mixed response, blacks moved steadily last year toward the concept that the only way to get fundamental change in city hall is to run it. In cities with or nearing black majorities, that is becoming a realistic possibility: Negro mayors have been elected in Cleveland and Gary, Ind., and appointed in Washington, D.C.; blacks already are organizing for the next municipal election in Newark. The total number of black elected officials in the country now is estimated at well over 800.[40] There are 389 in the South alone, an increase of 141 since February, 1968, largely spurred by the rise in Negro registration that has followed the federal voting rights law.[41] The total number of elected officials in the nation, however, is 520,000: The blacks thus hold .153 per cent of elected offices. They are just under 12 per cent of the population.

Having a Negro mayor does not automatically lead to the solution of ghetto problems. There remains the critical matter of resources to effect change, the shortage of which may produce even larger frustrations if a black man is put in charge and doesn't deliver. There is also a whole new set of communications barriers with the whites as outs (and for any mayor moderate enough to be elected, with more militant blacks as well). Carl B. Stokes of Cleveland, the nation's first elected Negro big-city mayor, last year moved on both fronts. In May, he announced the "Cleveland: Now!" program to spend $177 million in 18 months on problems of housing, jobs, health, and welfare. Most of the money was to come from anticipated federal grants, but private contributions were sought too. Business was asked to put up $10 million in ten days and did.

The July carnage was a severe blow to Cleveland Now and to Mayor Stokes. In the disorder which followed, Mayor Stokes pulled all white police out and asked the community to cool itself. His action caused deep and lasting bitterness on the force and resulted in a protracted feud in which much of the white middle class aligned with the police. Mayor Stokes is trying to heal this with a series of "town meetings," informal and well-attended, in which he tries to reassure the whites that his administration and Cleveland Now are serving their interests too. He has succeeded in holding much of the business support mustered for Cleveland Now, which dipped after the July killings.

From his election in November to July, Mayor Stokes had won an estimated $150 million in federal commitments to his city for housing, urban renewal, employment, and poverty programs. It was a far larger score than that of the previous administration: Urban renewal funds for Cleveland had been cut off entirely because of the city government's slowness. This part of the Stokes history underscores what was, by 1968, a significant fact: The federal government had entered the dialogue between city hall and the ghetto, and its voice was by no means neutral.

This is not a new phenomenon, of course, but it has grown with the number of federal programs and the fiscal needs of cities. The first direct federal effort of any scale to alter the relationship between city hall and the ghetto came in the community action program of the War on Poverty, which began by requiring "maximum feasible participation" of the poor in deployment of its dollars and wound up, to the delight of some and the dismay of others, encouraging the minority poor to become a conscious political force. Community action, for example, established some 700 neighborhood centers to dispense federally funded services in the coordinated way which the Commission advocated. In the past year, by the testimony of a community action official pleased with the fact, the corporations have shown less interest in coordinating services and more in accruing enough power to bring basic community change.

Among the dismayed were many mayors, who saw in the program federal money being used to fight city hall. The 90th Congress passed the so-called Green Amendment, which supporters of community action saw as an open invitation to mayors to take control of local programs. It has not worked out that way so far: The Office of Economic Opportunity engaged a consultant to survey 1,012 community action agencies on the impact of the amendment, and of 913 which responded 883 reported no substantial change in their structures or operations, according to a preliminary analysis of the figures. Most mayors apparently were satisfied with the workings of community action—or judged that the drive for destiny control among the minority poor had gained too much momentum to be challenged.

The future scale of the community action program was in some doubt as the Nixon Administration began. Attention had turned to the newer model cities program, which contains stringent requirements for citizen participation in its every stage. Model cities, however, has reserved a major role for city hall: The mayor has the responsibility for making the program, and citizen participation, work.

In late 1968, an internal report of the Model Cities Administration reviewed the first six months of community organization under the program. Many cities, it said, "may be moving toward confrontations and acrimony." Often, militant blacks in model neighborhoods initially said "no control, no participation"; in some this is proving negotiable but in others the militants are staying out and accusing the model cities community board of being "unrepresentative." On the other hand, the city hall that seeks only "the appearance of participation" is the norm rather than the exception, the report said: Often participation is defined "as the engineering of the consent of the governed."

"An equally disturbing issue" the report continued, "is the proliferation of citizen participation structures and advisory bodies in most cities." In every city involved in the program, there were at least two other citizens' bodies—for urban renewal, for health programs, for community action—before model cities came along. Moreover, many of the same citizens on these other boards turned up in the model cities structure. There were frequent difficulties getting model cities boards together because of competing meetings. "The proliferation of advisory and decision-making groups, and the creation of a segment of the poor or marginal population whose life is a whirlwind of public meetings, does not necessarily ensure a more sophisticated planning process," the report said. (On the other hand, "the growth of new civic institutions in low-income neighborhoods may be an indication that these areas are coming to resemble more affluent communities.")[42]

One intent of the model cities program is to achieve greater coordination of federal programs for human and physical renewal of the ghetto, and to get cities, through the carrot of federal aid, to do the same. The early experience of model cities, and of predecessor pilot neighborhood centers programs, has only served to underscore the difficulty of the task. "The federal government has not developed effective means to coordinate its present urban program, nor does it even understand completely the effects of its current activities in the city," Jay Janis, former executive assistant to the Secretary of HUD, wrote in September. "So far there is no real evidence that local governments can pull together the various elements needed to organize a comprehensive program of urban development." [43]

The significance of Janis's pessimism is that he was closely involved with the pulling together of the pilot neighborhood centers program, a 14-city attempt to create the kind of one-step dispensaries of services that the Commission specifically recommended. The program has seriously floundered at both the federal and local ends. Of the 14 attempts, the program's administrators can only point to five cities—Cincinnati, Louisville, Minneapolis, New York, and Chattanooga—as having made genuine progress. Of these, Cincinnati has come closest to the original concept of integrating welfare, employment, health, and other services in a single location with "outreach" to the community. The major problem in other cities was difficulty in getting local agencies to work with each other and with federal administrators. Except for construction money and OEO funds to the seven centers run by neighborhood corporations, there was no extra federal carrot in the program to convince local agencies they should yield some prerogatives.

At the federal end, interagency cooperation often turned instead into a wrangle, according to one program official. Involved were HUD, OEO, Labor, and Health, Education, and Welfare. HEW and Labor could not see that their program funds went to the centers because some are delivered through the states by formula. OEO's emphasis on community action rankled some of the other departments. HUD was supposed to do the co-ordinating, but as a sibling of the other departments—and a youngster at that—had difficulties making its views stick.

The end results of the programs were mostly negative lessons: how not to do it. Janis hopes model cities will show how to do it. But the situation has been further complicated in the past year by the increasing volume of black voices saying they want to do it all themselves.

8. Black Militancy, White Reaction

Detroit escaped disorder in April, 1968. Mayor Jerome Cavanagh declared a state of emergency after a series of demonstrations, centered in the schools, and they did not grow. To the *Inner-City Voice,* "Detroit's Black Community Newspaper," the mayor had made the city "a huge concentration camp, patrolled by caravans of killer cops and national guardsmen who allowed no respect for life." An editorial said, "It is only a few short steps from turning the city into a concentration camp to turning the local incinerators into crematoriums. The time to act is NOW. We must continue to prepare for what is more and more obviously an inevitable war developing from irreconcilable conflicts between the white rulers of this country and the black semi-slave in it. It may soon become illegal for you to purchase a weapon in this town. Have you got yours yet?"

The Commission heard such voices in 1967. They were, it said, "the ugly background noise of the violent summer." They have grown louder in the past year.

But there have been other voices, including that of the National Association for the Advancement of Colored People. In November, its official publication *The Crisis* spoke out against "this swaggering band of extremists." Said an editorial, "This nihilistic minority professes disdain for all 'white' values while at the same time invoking and utilizing, as instruments of controversy, the worst practices of the most benighted stratum of white society, to wit, obscene name-calling, threats, intimidation, suppression of opposing views, and violence." As for the call to revolution, "any revolution remotely possible in this country at this time . . . would be a revolution of the Right suppressing not only the black community but also curtailing the basic liberties of the total society."

Somewhere in a spectrum between readiness for revolution and acceptance of the system, between advocacy of complete separation from white society and belief in the goal and possibility of integration, is to be found the current mood of the nation's blacks. The indicators seem to have moved toward militancy in the past year, but there is ample room for such movement short of the extreme: Black pride need not mean black racism; separatism can be a means rather than an end, a way of "getting things together" so blacks can negotiate their place in society more as equals in strength; black rage can turn to constructive action rather than violence.

Precisely where the indicators stand now is impossible to say. The Commission was convinced, at the time of its report, that the civil disorders were far from being part of a revolutionary movement. "The central thrust of Negro protest in the current period has aimed at the inclusion of Negroes on a basis of full equality, rather than at a fundamental transformation of American institutions," it said. "There have been elements calling for a revolutionary overthrow of the American social system or for a complete withdrawal of Negroes from

American society. But these solutions have had little popular support. Negro protest, for the most part, has been firmly rooted in the basic values of the American society, seeking not their destruction but their fulfillment."

The Commission dismissed Black Power somewhat archly as "old wine in new bottles." To date, it said, "the evidence suggests that the situation is much like that of the 1840's, when a small group of intellectuals advocated slave insurrections, but stopped short of organizing them." At the same time, the Commission's picture of the "typical" 1967 rioter included these characteristics: "He takes great pride in his race and believes that in some respects Negroes are superior to whites. He is extremely hostile to whites, but his hostility is more apt to be a product of social and economic class than of race; he is almost equally hostile toward middle-class Negroes." His age was between 15 and 24.

Like every similar survey before it, one taken for the Commission and released in July, 1968, supported the assertion that blacks want in, not out, of the American system. It was the work of the Survey Research Center at the University of Michigan, and involved a cross-sectional sample of more than 5,000 Negroes and whites in 15 cities.[44] A total of 10 questions asked the blacks related to separatism vs. integration: Those favoring the separatist position on the 10 questions ranged from 5 to 18 per cent. Three questions related to the use of violence as a tactic: Those approving ranged from 6 to 15 per cent. "The most apparent fact," said the survey report, "is that the mood is not yet revolutionary. The great majority do not propose to withdraw from America; they want equal status in it. They do not talk of tearing down the economic and political institutions of the nation; they seek to share equally in the benefits."

Not all of the report was so comforting. A third of the respondents, it said, "believe discrimination in employment and housing are major facts of life for Negroes today, facts of life that are not getting much better." Within this third is the smaller group—"small but not trivial in numbers"—who feel violence to be necessary to achieve change. This group has "the sympathy and perhaps to some extent the support of the larger minority discussed above. The most important fact about those inclined toward violence is that they are not an isolated band of deviants condemned by almost all other Negroes, but are linked to a much larger group by a common definition of the problems that beset the Negro in America."

The report also suggested that the separatists also may have strength beyond their numbers. "To deviate from a very widely held norm probably requires more conviction than to hold to it," the researchers said. The concentration of blacks in the cities gives them "easy access to just the audience they wish to reach." The young, in particular, are listening. The percentage of teenage Negroes who believe in a separate black nation (11) was more than double the percentage of their elders. Nearly a third of the teenagers said they were ready to use violence to gain their rights. The survey found a similar acceptance of violence among young whites, and the report suggested that it may be explainable "in terms of a conception of teenage masculine daring that has little to do with race." It may also mean the rise of a truly revolutionary generation; the report acknowledged that the survey offered no way to tell.

The most hopeful part of the survey was an indication that the black community was making a distinction between the negative and positive aspects of Black Power: violence and separatism on the one hand, pride and identity on the other. While 80 per cent of the black respondents disagreed that all ghetto stores should be Negro owned, 94 per cent said that there should be more Negro businesses and 70 per cent that they should be favored by Negro customers. Ninety-six per cent said that "Negroes should take more pride in Negro history." And 42 per cent said that "Negro school children should study an African language," striking support, the report said, for a proposition "which a few years ago was scarcely discussed by most Negroes and still seems exotic and impractical to most white ears."

The assertion of black identity, the report said, is something quite different from separatism, and well within the tradition of American pluralism. "This seems to turn not so much on the rejection of whites as on the acceptance of things black," the report continued. "It involves a commitment to the development of Negro identity as a valid basis for cultural life within a larger interracial and if possible integrated society."

In early September, an Opinion Research Corporation survey for the Columbia Broadcasting System substantially confirmed the University of Michigan conclusions: Large majorities of blacks reject separatism and violence, but there is a rapid growth of black pride.[45] These two facts are consistent with a theory being cautiously advanced by some close observers of the events of the past year. They join the decline in civil disorder (excepting April for its tragic cause) to the rising emphasis on black self-help and community control. Incidents, especially police incidents, will continue to cause trouble. But the trouble will not be blown into full-scale disorder because people who are trying to build up their community don't want to see it destroyed.

This was the conclusion, again cautious and pro-tem, reached by a two-part series in *The New York Times* by Thomas A. Johnson. "The brother is too busy getting his thing together to think about riots," Tommy Jacquette of the SLANT organization in Watts told the *Times.* Said Robert Tindal, head of the NAACP in Detroit, "There is a new sophistication here. Negroes saw it was black people who died in the riots, but still they will not allow police to abuse them as they have in the past."

Others confirmed the conclusion in response to a *Wall Street Journal* survey by Monroe W. Karmin. Walter Bremond, chairman of the Black Congress of Los Angeles, one of a series of black-unity "umbrella" organizations formed in 1968: "The struggle has moved to a higher level. Blacks just won't get involved in fire-bombing and looting anymore. . . . The thrust now is to organize the black community at every level. . . ." The Rev. Curtis Burrell, chairman of Chicago's New Expanded Kenwood-Oakland Community Organization: "There isn't time for violence; we're too busy to engage in destructive activities." Joe Boyd, a Denver militant: "I don't think we could stand any large-scale rioting because we're too organized now, and the organization would fall."

But there were dissents, and warnings. "I don't think the lessening of violence this summer was because of anything that was done," said Kenneth Clark of the Metropolitan Applied Research Corporation. "And without fundamental changes in our society, any incident could trigger new violence." Detroit militant leader Rev. Dr. Albert Cleage agreed with the *Times* analysis of summer: "Black people here are just too busy for rioting, for throwing molotov cocktails." But he added that "the real danger of rebellion now, as in the past, depends on the white man."

The white man doesn't see things the same way as the black. The University of Michigan survey showed a wide divergence in black-white views on the crucial question of why the civil disorders had happened. Asked whether the disorders had been planned, 48.5 per cent of the whites answered in the affirmative (against 18 per cent of the blacks). Asked to cite the main cause of the disorders, 34 per cent of the whites named "looters and other undesirables" and 23.5 per cent "Black Power or other radicals"; 48.5 of the blacks named discrimination and other unfair treatment. Asked whether the disorders had helped or hurt "the cause of the Negro rights," 64 per cent of the whites said they had hurt, mostly on the grounds that they had increased "anti-Negro sentiments." The blacks' answer to the same question was mixed: A third said the disorders had helped, 23 per cent that they had hurt, and 24.5 per cent that they had not made any difference.

Perhaps the most revealing set of responses involved the relative position of whites and Negroes in the respondents' cities. The whites were asked whether Negroes with the same level of education as their own were relatively better or worse off than they. Forty-two per cent said better off and 46 per cent about the same; only 5 per cent said worse. The interviewers then cited figures showing that Negroes had worse jobs, education, and housing, and asked why the white respondents thought that was so. Nineteen per cent said it was because of discrimination, 56 per cent said it was "mainly due to something about the Negroes themselves," and 19 per cent thought it was a mixture of both. Two-thirds of the whites who thought the problem was inherent, however, thought the Negroes could be changed. Two-thirds of all the white respondents said that if government officials recommended programs to improve the living conditions of Negroes as necessary to prevent riots, they would go along. Fifty-three per cent said they would go along even if it meant a 10 per cent tax increase.

The University of Michigan findings, in other words, were mixed. The same could be said of other indicators of white reaction to blacks, to slum-ghetto problems, and to civil disorders in the year since the Commission report. Differences could be discerned, however, between white response at the beginning of the year and at the end, and between economic classes of whites.

The Commission report itself was received with loud official silence. It was released without White House ceremony, and Administration comment was scant. Press coverage was widespread, however (and press coverage of the slums and ghettos, criticized in the report, improved noticeably during 1968). A paperback version of the report sold an eventual 1.7 million copies. A Louis Harris poll just after its release found general agreement with many of the report's recommendations, but there were two points of white dissent: 53 per cent of the white respondents did not concur in the finding that "the riots were brought on mainly by white racism," and 59 per cent refused to believe they were not organized.

The nation suffered its first major trauma of 1968 with the assassination of Martin Luther King and the second followed immediately with the subsequent disorders. Dr. King was a respected figure among large numbers of white Americans—as he was preeminently admired by blacks—and his death caused the April disorders to be viewed with more understanding, although no less fear, than those of 1967. Combined with the Commission report, this sympathy brought a wave of anguished reaction summarized in the question "What can I do?" Individuals sought a role in easing the evident domestic crisis through volunteer efforts (no longer so welcome in the striving slums and ghettos as they once had been). There was a noticeable surge in response by the major religious faiths, business, and the unions, already activated by the 1967 disorders; and by private organizations from the American Bankers Association, the American Bar Association, the U.S. Jaycees and U.S. Chamber of Commerce to the League of Women Voters of the United States.

Another profound shock struck America in June with the killing of Sen. Robert F. Kennedy. After what had gone before, it seemed too much to bear. The national reaction took in all forms of violence, all kinds of turmoil. A Harris poll, the same month, on contributors to violence had "radicals who create violence on the street" at the head of the list and in third place "racial conflict in America"; the two were cited by 83 per cent and 76 per cent of those questioned, respectively. America wanted an end to violence, period: Something was happening to the country that no one could satisfactorily explain. (The President appointed the Commis-

9. Ghettos and Growth

In the long run, and in the Commission's terms, the significant question is not whether black-white polarization will cause disorders next summer but whether it will become a permanent American institution. There is one point on which one group each of blacks and whites are in agreement, namely the black separatists and the white segregationists: Both want blacks to remain in the inner-city neighborhoods where they are now, the blacks for power and the whites for protection.

Even if such an arrangement could bring racial peace, the Commission presumably would argue against it. In the first place, the Commission would point out (and did in its report), that it would mean the permanent disadvantagement of the black population: Jobs are trending toward the suburbs (between 75 and 80 per cent of added employment in trade and industry alone is going there), capital is in the hands of the white economy, separate schools are historically unequal, and in-city housing choices will continue to be limited. Secondly, and more importantly, the Commission would and did argue from the self-interest of the larger society. It made its recommendations, it said, "not to meet the needs of rioters or Negroes or, indeed, of any minority. We propose them to fulfill our pledge of equality and to meet the fundamental needs of a democratic and civilized society—domestic peace, social justice, and urban centers that are citadels of the human spirit." An American divided along racial lines, the Commission was saying, is not the kind of America its members wanted to live in.

Underlying all other forms of division is the simple spatial separation between the places where blacks and whites reside. Confinement of the blacks to the inner cities is what makes their neighborhoods ghettos, but even if they lived there voluntarily it would undercut possibilities for black-white contact and therefore social unity. As it is, a sense of confinement exacerbates all of the other problems that afflict these neighborhoods, by testimony of Kenneth Clark and others.

They became ghettos, the Commission said in its report, as a result of historic demographic changes which occurred throughout the century and intensified in postwar years. The first was the flow of Negroes from the South which began in World War I, continued in the years thereafter as Southern farms were mechanized, slowed in the Depression, and increased in World War II and through the 1950's. Also, by mid-century the Negro proportion of the total population had begun to grow as a result of higher birth rates for Negro women than whites and a sharper decline in death rates for Negroes than whites.

The Commission identified three streams of Negro migration: along the Atlantic Seaboard toward Boston, north from Mississippi toward Chicago, west from Texas and Louisiana toward California. The destination was the city. From 1950 to 1966, the Commission reported, 98 per cent of the increase in the Negro population of America occurred in metropolitan areas—86 per cent within central cities. By the time of the Commission report, the nation's 12 largest cities contained a third of its Negro population.

At the same time, another shorter-range migration was taking place: Whites were leaving the cities for the suburbs. From 1950 to 1966, 77.8 per cent of the white population increase was suburban; since 1960, the Commission reported, white central city population had declined by 1.3 million.

In 1968, the Douglas Commission published a report by two University of Chicago demographers, Patricia Leavey Hodge and Philip M. Hauser, which drew a straight-line projection of population trends from 1960 to 1985.[46] The report indicates that in the 25 years, central cities would lose 2.4 million whites, a 5 per cent decrease, and gain 10 million nonwhites, a 94 per cent increase. The suburbs would gain 53.9 million whites, a 104 per cent increase, and 4 million nonwhites—bringing their percentage of suburban population to between 5 and 6 per cent. The report commented, "The projections vividly portray the geographic fulfillment of the fears expressed by the President's Commission on Civil Disorders—that the American society is becoming an apartheid society. If the geographic separation of white and nonwhite occurs as projected, America by 1985 would be well on the road towards a society characterized by race stratification along social and economic lines . . ."

The report then adds two footnotes: The central city labor force would have to absorb a 112 per cent increase in the number of young nonwhite workers by 1985. Central city schools would have to accommodate an increase of 92 per cent in nonwhite youngsters under 15 (while losing 8 per cent of the whites in the same age group).

The authors emphasize that their figures are projections rather than predictions; that is, they are capable of being changed by events and policies. In the past year there has been significant change, but not entirely for the better.

Its direction was described for this review by Dr. Herman Miller, chief of the population division of the Census Bureau. "One of the things that has happened since the riots is that the rate at which whites are leaving the city has accelerated sharply," Dr. Miller said. "Before 1966 they moved at an average rate of 140,000 a year. Between 1966 and 1968 the rate climbed to nearly a half-million a year.

"The rate at which Negroes are moving into central cities decreased even more dramatically," he continued. "From 1960 to 1966, Negro population in central cities grew an average of 370,000 per year. In the past two years, however, growth has dropped to only about 100,000 per year and can be attributed largely to natural increase. Sampling variability prohibits an unqualified statement regarding trends of Negro migration to the suburbs. The data show, however, that the number of Negroes moving to the suburbs has increased from 20,000 per year before 1966 to 220,000 per year for the past two. Even so, he observed, "we're probably not getting much integration." [47]

The vision of a suburb usually includes a detached house with a green lawn and perhaps two cars in the garage. But in census terms, a suburb is any community within a metropolitan area and outside of the central city. This can include semi-rural Negro enclaves, such as dot suburban Montgomery County, Md., outside of Washington, and it can include slum-ghettos, such as exist in adjacent Prince Georges County, Md., just across the Washington line. The suburban slum-ghetto is becoming a visible, although unmeasured, phenomenon in many large metropolitan areas, particularly those around the older cities. (Planner Charles Abrams believes there are no longer any "suburbs" in the traditional sense in the inner rings around cities such as New York; they have become small cities with characteristic urban problems.)

There is some reason to believe that the increasing outward movement of Negroes from the cities does not entirely represent movement into the middle class and consequent achievement of suburban greenery: Much of it may represent a change from an urban ghetto to a suburban ghetto, and often the suburban ghetto may also be a slum. In 1967, median Negro family income in cities and suburbs differed by only $234 per year.[48] Thirty per cent of central city Negroes lived in poverty; so did 28 per cent of the Negroes in the suburbs.

Back in the city, meanwhile, the ghettos appear to be expanding in area as their population thins out. Real Estate Research Corporation each year tabulates Negro migration trends within Chicago. From 1960 to 1966, an average of 3.5 blocks per week shifted from predominantly white to nonwhite occupancy, mainly at the edge of nonwhite neighborhoods. In 1967 the figure dropped to 2.9—and in 1968 soared to 5.1. "Statements of ghetto dispersion," says the corporation's Anthony Downs, "are in large part due to the shifting boundaries of the ghetto." [49]

A Census Bureau study of the poverty neighborhoods of central cities in large metropolitan areas (over 250,000 population) found that: "White families left central city poverty areas at a faster rate than nonwhites between 1960 and 1968, resulting in an increase in the percentage of poverty area families who were nonwhite. There was a 35 per cent decline in the number of white families residing in poverty areas of large cities as compared with a drop of only 10 per cent in the number of nonwhite families." While white population declined throughout the 7-year period, ". . . the reduction for nonwhite families took place only between 1967 and 1968."[50] The thinning out of population, moreover, did not necessarily mean progress: It is predictable in deteriorating areas because of demolition or condemnation of dilapidated housing units and the low rate of replacement, according to the bureau's report.

In testimony before Congress on the Housing Act of 1968, economist George Sternlieb of Rutgers University took a closer look at the phenomenon. "A new pattern is evolving," he said. "This involves whole areas of hard-core slums which are becoming depopulated. These are areas in which no new immigrant group can be found; for which, in an age of welfare, no group is desperate enough. . . . In Newark, for example, the gross vacancy rate in the 25 hard-core slum tracts is 14 per cent." He called it "a situation of dynamic degeneration," with "high vacancy rates making for even higher vacancy rates," even in cities with sizable housing shortages as blight and abandonment spread.[51]

It is not an appealing picture of the urban future.

10. Conclusions

"The deepening racial division is not inevitable," the Commission said a year ago. "The movement apart can be reversed. Choice is still possible. Our principal task is to define that choice and to press for a national resolution." The following summarizes the national response to that task in relation to the issues examined in the preceding pages.

1. Civil disorders increased in number but declined in intensity in 1968. A significant drop in the death rate was due primarily to more sophisticated response by police and the military, resulting directly from the work of the Commission.

2. A wave of disorder struck the nation's high schools in 1968–69 and is continuing. At the same time, turbulence on college and university campuses has taken on an increasingly racial character.

3. A genuinely alarming increase in crimes of violence contributed to an atmosphere of fear inside and out of the slums and ghettos. There was little evidence of change or reform in the criminal justice system sufficient to stem this increase.

4. Incidents involving the police continued to threaten the civil peace in the slums and ghettos. There was some evidence of a hardening of police attitudes and

a weakening of traditional civil controls over their activities.

5. Structural change in local government to make it more responsive was rare. The number of black elected officials increased substantially throughout the nation and particularly in the South, but remained disproportionately low.

6. There was no evidence that any more than a small minority of the nation's Negro population was prepared to follow militant leaders toward separatism or the tactical use of violence. This minority, however, continued to have an impact beyond its numbers, particularly on the young.

7. There was striking evidence of a deepening of the movement toward black pride, black identity, and black control and improvement of ghetto neighborhoods. There were repeated suggestions that efforts toward community control and self-help had been a major contribution to the relative quiet of the summer, 1968.

8. White concern with the problems of the slums and ghettos mounted with the Commission report, the assassination of Martin Luther King, and the April disorders. It was subsumed by concern for law and order in the months following the assassination of Sen. Robert F. Kennedy, and continued to decline during the Presidential campaign. Outright resistance to slum-ghetto needs and demands intensified during the same months.

9. Black and white Americans remained far apart in their perception of slum-ghetto problems and the meaning of civil disorders. The gap probably had widened by the end of the year.

10. The physical distance between the places where blacks and whites lived did not diminish during the

past year and threatens to increase with population growth. The most recent trend showed a virtual stoppage in black immigration and a sharp increase in the rate of white departure; the ghettos, meanwhile, were growing in area while declining in population density. There was an increase in suburban Negro population, but there also were indications of growth in suburban ghettos.

The nation has not reversed the movement apart. Blacks and whites remain deeply divided in their perceptions and experiences of American society. The deepening of concern about conditions in the slums and ghettos on the part of some white persons and institutions has been counterbalanced—perhaps overbalanced—by a deepening of aversion and resistance on the part of others. The mood of the blacks, wherever it stands precisely in the spectrum between militancy and submission, is not moving in the direction of patience. The black neighborhoods in the cities remain slums, marked by poverty and decay; they remain ghettos, marked by racial concentration and confinement. The nation has not yet made available—to the cities or the blacks themselves—the resources to improve these neighborhoods enough to make a significant change in their residents' lives. Nor has it offered those who might want it the alternative of escape.

Neither has the nation made a choice among the alternative futures described by the Commission, which is the same as choosing what the Commission called "present policies." The present policies alternative, the Commission said, "may well involve changes in many social and economic programs—but not enough to produce fundamental alterations in the key factors of Negro concentration, racial segregation, and the lack of sufficient enrichment to arrest the decay of deprived neighborhoods."

It is worth looking again at the Commission's description of where this choice would lead:

"We believe that the present policies choice would lead to a larger number of violent incidents of the kind that have stimulated recent major disorders.

"First, it does nothing to raise the hopes, absorb the energies, or constructively challenge the talents of the rapidly growing number of young Negro men in central cities. The proportion of unemployed or underemployed among them will remain very high. These young men have contributed disproportionately to crime and violence in cities in the past, and there is danger, obviously, that they will continue to do so.

"Second, under these conditions, a rising proportion of Negroes in disadvantaged city areas might come to look upon the deprivation and segregation they suffer as proper justification for violent protest or for extending support to now isolated extremists who advocate civil disruption by guerrilla tactics.

"More incidents would not necessarily mean more or worse riots. For the near future, there is substantial likelihood that even an increased number of incidents could be controlled before becoming major disorders, if society undertakes to improve police and National Guard forces so that they can respond to potential disorders with more prompt and disciplined use of force.

"In fact, the likelihood of incidents mushrooming into major disorders would be only slightly higher in the near future under the present policies choice than under the other two possible choices. For no new policies or programs could possibly alter basic ghetto conditions immediately. And the announcement of new programs under the other choices would immediately generate new expectations. Expectations inevitably increase faster than performance. In the short run, they might even increase the level of frustration.

"In the long run, however, the present policies choice risks a seriously greater probability of major disorders, worse, possibly, than those already experienced.

"If the Negro population as a whole developed even stronger feelings of being wrongly 'penned in' and discriminated against, many of its members might come to support not only riots, but the rebellion now being preached by only a handful. Large-scale violence, followed by white retaliation, could follow. This spiral could quite conceivably lead to a kind of urban *apartheid* with semimartial law in many major cities, enforced residence of Negroes in segregated areas, and a drastic reduction in personal freedom for all Americans, particularly Negroes."

The Commission's description of the immediate consequences of the present policies choice sounds strikingly like a description of the year since its report was issued: some change but not enough; more incidents but less full-scale disorder because of improved police and military response; a decline in expectations and therefore in short-run frustrations. If the Commission is equally correct about the long run, the nation in its neglect may be sowing the seeds of unprecedented future disorder and division. For a year later, we are a year closer to being two societies, black and white, increasingly separate and scarcely less unequal.

References

1. U.S. Bureau of the Census, "Trends in Social and Economic Conditions in Metropolitan Areas," *Current Population Reports,* Series P-23, No. 27, February 7, 1969.
2. U.S. Department of Labor, Bureau of Labor Statistics, *The Employment Situation in Urban Poverty Neighborhoods: Fourth Quarter, 1968,* January 16, 1969.
3. *Ibid.*
4. U.S. Department of Labor, Bureau of Labor Statistics, *Employment and Earnings and Monthly Report on the Labor Force,* Vol. 15, No. 7, January 1969.
5. U.S. Equal Employment Opportunity Commission, "Job Patterns for Minorities and Women in Private Industry, 1966," *Equal Employment Opportunity Report No. 1,* Government Printing Office, 1968.
6. Annual Report of the Council of Economic Advisers, in the "Economic Report of the President," January, 1969.
7. *Ibid.*
8. Ad hoc hearings on Discrimination in Employment, Rep. William F. Ryan, Chairman, December 3–5, 1968.
9. Hubert H. Humphrey, "The Right to Succeed: Minority Entrepreneurship," Statement in Washington, D.C., July 20, 1968.
10. Sen. Charles H. Percy, "Building the New America," at American Management Association briefing session, New York: "Developing Practical Programs for Enterprise in the Ghetto: The New Capitalism," December 18, 1968.

11. Milton Moskowitz, "Where It's At: Black Capitalism," *Business and Society,* I, No. 13, December 17, 1968.
12. Howard Greenberg, Deputy Administrator of the Small Business Administration, at the American Management Association briefing session, New York: Developing Practical Programs for Enterprise in the Ghetto: The New Capitalism," December 18, 1968.
13. Moskowitz, *op. cit.*
14. Small Business Administration, "Development of Minority Business Ownership," January, 1969. (mimeo.)
15. Interview with Maurice Ellis, Statistical Services Branch, National Center for Social Statistics, Department of Health, Education, and Welfare, February, 1969.
16. Interview with Robert Carroll, Assistant to Jack R. Goldberg, Commissioner of Social Services, New York, February, 1969.
17. Department of Health, Education, and Welfare, "Source of Funds for Public Assistance Payments," June 30, 1968.
18. *The New York Times,* October 14, 1968.
19. Regional Plan Association, *Public Services in Older Cities,* New York City, May, 1968.
20. U.S. Bureau of the Census, *op. cit.*
21. Interview with George Wiley, head of the Washington office, National Welfare Rights Organization, February, 1969.
22. Interview with Andrew Truelson, Assistant Director for Special Services, Welfare Administration, Department of Health, Education, and Welfare, February, 1969.
23. Luvern L. Cunningham and Raphael O. Nystrand, "Citizen Participation in School Affairs: A Report to the Urban Coalition," Ohio State University, November, 1968. (mimeo.)
24. U.S. Office of Education, "More Effective Schools, New York City," Government Printing Office, 1969.
25. U.S. Office of Education, "Profiles in Quality Education," Government Printing Office, 1968.

26. Office of Education estimate.
27. The National Advisory Council on the Education of Disadvantaged Children, "Title I-ESEA," Fourth Annual Report, Government Printing Office, 1969.
28. The President's Committee on Urban Housing, Edgar F. Kaiser, Chairman, "A Decent Home," Government Printing Office, 1969; and The National Commission on Urban Problems, Paul H. Douglas, Chairman, "Building the American City," Government Printing Office, 1969.
29. National Commission on Urban Problems, *op. cit.*
30. Council of Economic Advisers, *op. cit.*
31. George Schermer Associates, "More than Shelter: Social Needs in Low- and Moderate-Income Housing," *Research Report No. 8,* prepared for The National Commission on Urban Problems, Government Printing Office, 1968.
32. Institute of Public Administration, "Rapid Rehabilitation of Old Law Tenements: An Evaluation," New York City, September, 1968.
33. International City Managers Association, *Urban Data Service,* Vol. I, No. 1, January, 1969.
34. National Commission on the Causes and Prevention of Violence, "Progress Report to President Lyndon B. Johnson," January 9, 1969.
35. Lemberg Center for the Study of Violence, *Riot Data Review,* No. 2, August, 1968.
36. Federal Bureau of Investigation, *Uniform Crime Reporting,* January–September, 1968.
37. Interview with Captain Ralph Stines, Commanding Officer, Robbery Division, D.C. Police Department, February, 1969.
38. Advisory Commission on Intergovernmental Relations, *Tenth Annual Report,* Washington, D.C., January 31, 1969.
39. Gary T. Marx, "Report of the National Commission: The Analysis of Disorder or Disorderly Analysis?" 1968. (mimeo.)

40. Estimates from the Democratic and Republican National Committees.
41. Figures from the Voter Education Project, Southern Regional Council, Atlanta, Georgia.
42. Department of Housing and Urban Development, "Citizen Participation in Model Cities: Development, Dynamics, and Dilemmas During the First Six Months," September 16, 1968. (draft)
43. Jay Janis, "Model Cities: Their Role Is Vital in Developing an Overall Urban Strategy," *Nation's Cities,* Vol. 6, No. 9, September, 1968.
44. Supplemental Studies for the National Advisory Commission on Civil Disorders, July, 1968.
45. "Black America" series, concluding portion, September 2, 1968.
46. "The Challenge of America's Metropolitan Population Outlook, 1960–1985," prepared for the National Commission on Urban Problems, Patricia Leavey Hodge and Philip M. Hauser, *Research Report No. 3,* Government Printing Office, 1968.
47. Interview with Dr. Herman Miller, January 30, 1969.
48. U.S. Bureau of the Census, *op. cit.*
49. Interview with Dr. Anthony Downs, January, 1969.
50. U.S. Bureau of the Census, *op. cit.*
51. Statement by George Sternlieb, Research Director of the Graduate School of Business, Rutgers State University, before U.S. Senate Subcommittee on Housing and Urban Affairs of the Committee on Banking and Currency, 90th Congress, 2nd Session.

Rosengren's
BOOKS
SAN ANTONIO, TEXAS

HN
59
.U7